A Shropshire Squire

Miniatures of Noel Hill, Anne Hill,
and Henrietta, Anne and Emily. *(National Trust)*

A Shropshire Squire

Noel Hill, first Lord Berwick
1745-1789

Barbara Coulton

SWAN HILL
PRESS

Copyright © Barbara Coulton, 1989

British Library Cataloguing in Publication Data

Coulton, Barbara
    A Shropshire squire: Noel Hill, first Lord Berwick.
    1.   England. Rural regions. Gentry. Social life,
    history
    I.   Title
    942'.009'734

    ISBN 1 85310 092 7

First published in 1989 by Swan Hill Press,
an imprint of Airlife Publishing Ltd.

Printed in England.

Swan Hill Press

An Imprint of Airlife Publishing
101 Longden Road, Shrewsbury SY3 9EB, England.

Contents

Acknowledgements

I would like to thank all who helped me in this work: Miss Belinda Cousens of the National Trust; Mrs M T Halford, County Archivist, and staff at the Shropshire Record Office; Mr G C Baugh, Editor, the Victoria County History, Shropshire; Mr A M Carr and staff of the Local Studies Library, Shrewsbury; staff of other libraries and record offices, and individuals and institutions who are named in the notes on sources, at the end of the book.

I am also grateful to those who have given permission to use, and have provided, the illustrations for portraits at Attingham: the National Trust and the Courtauld Institute of Art; for objects at Attingham, the National Trust. For the portrait of Lady Henrietta Grosvenor, the Eaton Estate (Duke of Westminster). For the portrait of Sir Charlton Leighton, Sir Michael Leighton (photograph by Paul Stamper). For the drawings of Shrewsbury election 1774 and Attingham 1800, the Local Studies Library, Shrewsbury. For the Oswestry Race Cup, the Town Council of Oswestry. For the view of Hilton Hall, the William Salt Library, Stafford (photograph by Peter Rogers).

Introduction

There are two houses in Shropshire associated with the Hill family: that of Hawkstone is the older, the home of the senior branch of the family in the eighteenth century; while the great mansion of Attingham was built late in the century, by the most notable member of a younger branch — Noel Hill, first Lord Berwick. In each house there hangs a portrait of the Hon. Richard Hill, who inherited Hawkstone in 1700, on the death of his father Rowland, who is buried at nearby Hodnet. Richard enjoyed an urbane life in his homes in London and at Richmond, but he used his wealth to increase his Shropshire estates and to improve Hawkstone. He also bought the manor of Attingham or Atcham, a few miles south-east of Shrewsbury, and had a modest house built there — Tern Hall — for the nephew who represented the younger Shropshire branch of the family. He had his marble monument sent up to Hodnet, and devised the list of his achievements as envoy; he died in 1727, leaving Hawkstone to his nephew Rowland, the first baronet. Sir Rowland's additions to Hawkstone include the Saloon, where his portrait hangs. Of his five sons, the three youngest became clergymen, influenced by their eldest brother who was a noted religious controversialist. This brother was Richard, who became second baronet in 1783; the second brother, John, succeeded as third baronet; both were Members of Parliament. One of John's sons, Rowland, was the military hero who became Lord Hill, during the Napoleonic Wars; he it is whose statue adorns the famous Column, on the outskirts of Shrewsbury. But it is with the other Shropshire branch of the Hill family that this book is concerned.

The monument to their memory is Attingham itself, although the building of that house comes late in our story. First we follow the life of Richard Hill's nephew Thomas: son of a Shrewsbury grocer and of Hill's sister Margaret, his life was mapped out by his uncle, and he took the surname Hill. With the wealth he carefully accumulated he added to his Shropshire estates, and his influence brought him, in middle life, one of the Parliamentary seats for Shrewsbury. He remained more a man of business than a country squire, never as confident of his social status as his son was to be. His judicious second marriage gave his children a more prestigious lineage, so that his son Noel, with his Cambridge education and more 'genteel' tastes, took on the role of squire with aplomb. Though he achieved no eminence, he was in time ennobled — to a peerage, which caused chagrin at Hawkstone. His life, short though it was, provides us with an insight into the interests and way of life of a Georgian gentleman, and a Shropshire squire.

Barbara Coulton
May 1989

Chapter 1
Family and Childhood

Noel Hill was born on 16 April 1745, at 3 Cleveland Court, St James's, his family's London home; he was the fourth and last child of Thomas and Susanna Hill. Thomas Hill, by this time in his fifties, was a wealthy man of business with estates in Shropshire. The Hills of Hawkstone had been settled in that county for several generations, but Thomas was of a minor branch of

The Rt Hon Richard Hill of Hawkstone (d. 1727), uncle of Thomas Hill. *(Courtauld Institute)*

the family. His mother, Margaret, was sister of Richard Hill, Deputy Paymaster to the Army in Flanders in the reign of William III, and envoy in that reign and the reign of Queen Anne. Having made a fortune, Richard bought up estates in his native Shropshire, and undertook rebuilding at Hawkstone, although he preferred his homes in the south, at Cleveland Court and Richmond.

Although unmarried he wanted to ensure that the family name and fortunes survived, so he established three nephews as his successors. Rowland, son of his brother John, was heir to Hawkstone; he was left a fortune and a baronetcy was acquired for him, before Richard Hill's death in 1727. His sister Elizabeth's son, Samuel, was educated at Cambridge, given a sinecure in the Admiralty, and set up with an estate at Shenstone in Staffordshire. Margaret's son, Thomas, had a different education — eight years apprenticed to George Clifford, a leading banker in Holland. His father was Thomas Harwood, Margaret's second husband, a grocer and member of the Drapers' Company in Shrewsbury.

Thomas (Harwood) Hill of Tern (d. 1782), father of Noel Hill. *(Courtauld Institute)*

We know nothing of young Thomas's early life, probably spent with his parents in Shrewsbury; there was, apparently, a period at Eton (no records of this survive), and he was eighteen before his mercantile training abroad began. On his return to England in 1722 he was married to Anne Powys, daughter of a Clerk in the Treasury (Richard Hill was a Lord of the Treasury); Richard Powys was related to the Powys family of Berwick in Shropshire. An estate there had already been provided for Thomas (like his cousin Samuel, he adopted the name Hill) and Tern Hall built, near the village of Atcham; for some thirty years it was lived in by the Harwoods. Thomas' wife died in 1739; their son Richard had died when he was eleven, but two daughters survived, Ann and Margaret.

In 1740 Thomas Hill remarried: his second wife was barely twenty — Susanna Maria, daughter of William Noel, lawyer and M.P. for Stamford. The Noels of Kirkby Mallory in Leicestershire traced their pedigree in England back to the Conquest, and their baronetcy back to the Restoration. William was the second son of the fourth baronet, his brother, Clobery, succeeding. Susanna was one of four daughters — with Anne, Frances and Elizabeth, she was her father's co-heir. The first five years of her marriage produced four children: Susanna, 'Sukey', Maria, 'Molly', then the longed-for heir, Samuel, on 29 September 1743 (he was named after the rich and childless cousin of his father), and, finally, Noel, named after his mother's family. In the year of his birth his mother's cousin Sir Edward Noel succeeded also to the barony of Wentworth — this was a prominent aristocratic family in the north of England. The children's grandfather Noel assumed the prefix Honourable on his nephew's elevation. Pride in this side of the family, commemorated in Noel's name, was, in the next generation, to be marked by the assumption of the surname Noel-Hill.

This then was Noel's lineage. His own family seems to have been close and affectionate, despite Thomas Hill's age and his reserved character. When his son Samuel was born, Thomas's eldest daughter, Ann, who was staying at the Noels' home in Stamford, wrote to him: 'Dear Pappa, I trouble you with this to congratulate you upon the birth of my Brother which I believe gives you and my Mamma no small Joy . . . I think I never was so pleased with any news in my life as when I heard that my Mamma and the Child were both well and that it was a boy.' She and her sister Peggy doubtless welcomed Noel as warmly. It was Ann who wrote to Shropshire with the news. She often acted as amanuensis, copying her father's letters into his letter-book, and writing to the steward at Tern on a variety of matters. He replied on 20 April: 'I Recd Miss Hills with the good News of My Mistresses safe Delivery of a son of which I wish you much Joy and am very glad to hear My Mistress is in so hopefull a way . . . and hope she will soon be able to travell to Shropshire.'

Thomas Bell, a north country man, had been appointed steward at Tern in 1734, by Thomas Harwood, who could no longer look after his son's estate. Hill had shown little interest in the house at Tern, although keen to receive the rents from the estate, and Bell took good care of both. Susanna Hill had a more positive attitude and from her first visit in the summer of 1740 began to plan improvements to the garden and the house. Bell was her faithful agent. That September, when the family were back in London, he wrote to Hill: 'I will likewise take care that there shall be roses etc. planted in the walk in the Coppice . . . Edwd Jones desires to know whether you'l have the Ground laid out and planted with Paradice stocks.' The garrets were done up for children's rooms and nursery, and were being repainted when Noel was born. In that letter on 20 April Bell reported that the painter had finished the garrets and wanted to begin on the staircase, 'but I have made him hold his Hand 'till we have your orders and the sooner we have'm the better that it may be finished and dry against you come . . . I have ordered a Box of Cakes to be sent . . . of which I desire Miss Sukey, Miss Molly and Master Samuels acceptance and that may be equal shares therein.' (The cakes were probably Shrewsbury cakes.)

Bell was to be an important figure in the children's life at Tern, where they were taken each summer. His letters tell us little of his own affairs (once he mentions that his brother is visiting him from the north) but they contain much about estate business and Shropshire matters. In the winter after Noel's birth events on a national scale reverberated in the county. Prince Charles Edward, who had landed on Eriskay in July, led his army south, through Preston and Manchester to Macclesfield and then to Derby, where lack of support and the threat of Cumberland's forces made him retreat. Confused reports reach Shrewsbury. Bell had heard that the rebels were in Staffordshire and making for Shrewsbury; Lord Herbert's regiment was moving out of the town. Carts, waggons and coaches had been carrying things away most of the night, he wrote on 9 December, 'and the Town is in the Greatest Confusion ever known'. He was making arrangements to send the horses to safe places, but waited for more reliable reports. A man from Congleton assured him that the rebels had not been as close as rumoured, though some imaginative souls had claimed to have heard their drums. The fear subsided and the carts and waggons returned to town. Life resumed its normal course, and Bell sent to the Raven for the ornamental shells which had been sent by water — Mrs Hill had a passion for collecting these, as we shall see.

In London Thomas Hill was occupied with business and his wife was often alone, though her step-daughters would have provided companionship and help with the children. Once she wrote that she had been in all day, hoping for visitors to call with chit-chat. Occasionally she went to the theatre or the opera, or attended court. The summer brought the move to the country, and sometimes a visit to friends or to her home at Stamford. In the summer of 1748 she went to stay with Marmaduke and Sarah Gwynne at Garth in Breconshire; they enjoyed keeping open house. Susanna Hill wrote home to say that Lord Powis and his brother and Mr Francis Herbert had called on them during the Ludlow Races. 'The Race is over this evening but there is a Danceing Assembly tomorrow Night; and Friday it will be quite necessary to rest. And on Saturday I propose to return home to you and my Dear little ones . . . the Company waits for me to go to the Ball or I could gladly trouble you with a great deal more tittle-tattle.' In her thirtieth year, she still enjoyed such pastimes, though she was truly devoted to her family. An undated note to her husband, written at Tern while he was in Shrewsbury, reads: 'My Dear, I find Sammy is a good deal better this morning but Noel had a return of his fever yesterday and is not quite free from it at present: but I hope it is only occation'd by the extraordinary heat of the weather; if you can without giving offence get me excused dining at the Raven tomorrow I should be glad to stay at home and nurse the Boys.' More at ease in society than her husband, she was a good hostess, a great asset when he became M.P. for Shrewsbury and had to make more than business contacts.

Shrewsbury sent two members to Parliament. Since the election of 1734 these were Whigs: William Kynaston of Ruyton-XI-Towns (a graduate of St John's College, Cambridge and a Master in Chancery) and Sir Richard Corbett, first elected in 1722. There had been opposition in 1734, but in 1741 the two members were returned unopposed; in 1747 they beat two opposing candidates. By the end of 1748 news had reached Shrewsbury that the Master (as Bell calls Kynaston in his letters) was gravely ill. Godolphin Edwards, who had been Mayor in 1729, offered the Corporation's interest to John Mytton of Halston, who declined. Hill was then approached, and accepted; he had the support of both Mytton and Corbett. Kynaston did die, early in 1749; Bell wrote that the Corporation were disqualifying nearly forty burgesses to ensure a majority. He also commented on the importance of Lord Powis, the Recorder of Shrewsbury and Lord Lieutenant of the County: he was 'more absolute in this part of the world than the King of France is in his capital city'. In March Hill was duly selected in place of Kynaston; Bell paid the election bills of over £260. On 25 March Hill wrote from London to thank Mytton for appearing in person at the election. He had been to visit Mytton's son at his school in Fulham, and had invited Master Mytton (then aged about twelve) to stay at Cleveland Court for the Whitsuntide holiday, and to a firework display at St James's. There was some danger of smallpox, but if the boy fell ill Mrs Hill would nurse him tenderly. In the event it was Sukey and Molly who caught the illness, in a mild form.

The family stayed in Town until June, for a wedding. As early as February, Bell had been making disguised enquiries about the Burton family of Longner, neighbouring estate to Tern. There were two 'lunatick' sisters of the late Thomas Burton, but the affliction did not show itself in the male line. Robert Burton was to marry Ann Hill, a match probably of their own choosing, for Thomas Hill remarked in a letter to his cousin Sir Rowland: 'It seems this had been talked of some time before I knew anything of the matter in earnest.' Ann was twenty-three, with her own fortune left to her by her mother. She was married at St James's Chapel on 8 June; the bells were rung at Atcham; and Peggy accompanied the Burtons on their wedding journey.

Thomas Hill went briefly with his father-in-law to Cambridge, and his wife, alone with the children, wrote from Cleveland Court. 'I have been extreamly busie ever since seven this morning in order to be ready to set out for

The Hon William Hill (d.1762), grandfather of Noel Hill. *(Courtauld Institute)*

Shropshire when ever you return to Town . . . I thought it would be a pleasure to you to have the freshest advices of your Dear Boys: they are both in great spirits, tho the weather is still extream hot.' In Shropshire one of her closest friends was young Mrs Leighton. Anna Maria Mytton (a cousin of Master Mytton) had eloped in London in 1744 with Charlton Leighton, of Loton Park. She was very young and an heiress; her mother (Letitia Owen of Condover) was distraught, but they were reconciled. Mrs Barnston (she had remarried after the death of her first husband Richard Mytton) moved to

Susanna Maria (Noel) Hill (d. 1760), mother of Noel Hill. *(Courtald Institute)*

Bath for her health, and she and Anna Maria wrote to each other constantly. The Leightons' first child, also named Anna Maria, went to live with her grandmother. The second child was a son, Charlton, and two more girls followed, Honor and Belle. In the spring of 1750 Mrs Leighton often mentioned Mrs Hill in her letters. On 7 April she wrote from their home near Shrewsbury Abbey: 'Mrs Hill comes down the week after next which I am very glad of for it will be a good airing to go and see her a morning.' Young Charlton had recently been put into breeches and fancied himself quite a little man; he was a little younger than Noel Hill and the two boys formed a childhood friendship that was to be lifelong.

Charlton was also getting under people's feet at home and was sent during the day to a nearby dame's school, which he enjoyed. Once the Hills had come he would be able to accompany his mother on her airings and play with Noel and Sam at Tern. On 28 April, a Saturday, Anna Maria wrote to her mother at eight in the evening: 'Mr Leighton and I are just this moment come from Mrs Hills where we spent the day with Lord Powis Sir R^d and Mr Edward Corbett Sir H. Edwards and young Mr Fellows, his Lordship stays there till tomorrow morning in his way to London . . . [Mrs Hill] looks better than I ever saw her, but the eldest Miss [Peggy] is gone extream plain besides and is agreable.' On Tuesday 22 May she wrote: 'Mrs Hill and I see one another very often, she comes to drink tea with me this Evening and we go to the dancing assembly. She is not with child.' Mrs Hill's fears in this respect had proved groundless but Anna Maria was pregnant. She had written to her mother early in May: 'I wrote you word Mama as soon as ever I found I was breeding and reckon the middle of September.'

Another, undated, letter confirms the friendship with Susanna Hill. 'Mrs Hill came to me this morning at eight o'clock. I am to dine with her and she returns with me. She is one of the best neighbours that can be, for we see one another almost every day. Mr and Mrs Burton are coming to them soon.' Their interest in their children, and in music (Mr Burney was teaching Anna Maria the harpsichord), would have enhanced the companionship. Susanna Hill had a particular hobby, and made her friend a present: 'Mrs Hill has given me the prettiest peice of shellwork I ever saw I think it exceeds all she has yet made and I desire Mama you will oblige me in accepting of it . . . it is an Urn full of Flowers the shells extreamly small.' She was enjoying the 'charming weather' of early summer, but by July, 'I now grow much bigger and am troublesome to myself. Mrs Hill sent to me this morning [Saturday 7 July] to desire I would dine at her house to meet Lord and Lady Wentworth but I am not very well and could not go.' These new guests were Susanna Hill's cousin Sir Edward, and his wife Judith. Anna Maria was concerned that summer about her mother's health, assuring her in August that she herself was well, but, tragically, in that month Anna Maria died, aged twenty-three. (Her husband, left with young children and expensive tastes, remarried in 1751.)

Mrs Hill was not entirely free from illness, and in the summer of 1751 she and her husband went to the recently popular spa at Llandrindod. A Mr Grosvenor of Shrewsbury had converted Llandrindod Hall into a spacious hotel with one hundred beds, suites of rooms for concerts, balls and billiards, and shops for luxury items. Beyond were the beneficial springs, and walks and rides in lovely surroundings. While their parents were away, Sam and Noel were looked after at Tern by Thomas Bell. Noel was now six, and Samuel nearly eight, and the question of their education was being considered. Their mother and Margaret probably saw to basic requirements, like reading and writing, and they were encouraged by their father to learn French — some French servants were employed. More serious schooling was needed, however, perhaps at the school where Master Mytton had been sent.

In April 1751 Thomas wrote to his cousin Samuel: 'I am much oblig'd to you for the friendship by enquireing in your way [to Scarborough] after the schools of Burton and Ripton but they are at too great a distance & out of the line. I had a design to put my Boys under the care of Dr Croftes at Fulham but when I came to Town I found he was declining that Buisness: & that Mr Cox at Kinsington was grown past his usual attention to his young Scollars.' (Perhaps we should attribute the spelling mistakes to Margaret, who now copied her father's letters into the letter-book.) Hill was however governed by his wife in this matter. 'She had learned it from Mr Poyntz to prefer a private education, for the sake of grounding youth in the principles of Religion and Honor which he was used to say were rarely or never to be truly fixt afterwards.'

Mr Poyntz was probably Stephen Poyntz, celebrated tutor to the nobility, and diplomat. Mrs Hill did not want her sons sent yet to a 'great school' such as Eton or Westminster, so a private tutor was sought. On the return to London in the autumn of that year they heard of a young man, recommended by a Mr des Champs, who was suitable. He was Swiss, educated at the University of Geneva, and had been in England for over a year, at the school of a Mr Burchell in Hertfordshire. His name was Jean Guillaume de la Fléchère, which he anglicised for convenience to John Fletcher. In the autumn of 1751 he became tutor at Cleveland Court.

The following March, Fletcher wrote a long letter to his father in Nyon, to tell him of his appointment and of the family with whom he now lived. This gives us a rare and intriguing insight into the Hill household. Fletcher was a pious young man (he was twenty-two) and was happy that he had found a post in a home where he was not ridiculed. *'Je suis heureusement tombé dans une maison ou mon genre de vie loin de scandaliser, se fait plutot imiter que tourner en ridicule.'* 'Monsieur d'Hill', aged sixty (in fact fifty-eight), did not like display and showed little aptitude for human relationships. His time was taken up in business, walking, and reading; at home he always had a book in his hand — usually a grammar! Fletcher thought this passion strange, and inconvenient, since Hill wanted him to follow his example and teach this dry branch of *belles-lettres* to his charges. Hill's stay in Paris — he must have told the young man of the period abroad long ago when he travelled in France with a friend, James Bonnell — had given him another weakness: to rate highly only what originated from that city. This had nearly caused the ruin of his sons whom he had entrusted to someone *'aussi débauché qu'ignorant'* (perhaps a servant). Fletcher, however, counted on the boys' good nature and tender age to allow him to lead them back on the path of virtue. *'A l'égard de leurs études, leurs parens doivent être satisfaits, puisque dans 4 mois ils ont fait plus de progres qu'on n'en fait dans 18 dans les meilleures acadèmies de ce pays.'* Mrs Hill's views on great schools as opposed to private tutors was thus being vindicated. Fletcher evidently found his new *métier* hard work, but he chose to work too much rather than neglect his duty. This must have come as something of a shock to Sam and Noel. There was some leisure, when his pupils went dancing, or walking, or riding, with their mother. He had been invited to accompany them but declined, though he did take dancing lessons himself, in London. He also had friends among the Swiss community there.

Turning to Mrs Hill, Fletcher described her as *'une grosse et grande femme, qui a été fort belle'* — she was still handsome, he said. He considered that, without being clever, she had the taste and outlook of those who attended the court and assemblies. She had a taste for spending, while her husband's was for economy, but she had the secret of getting him to spend, to provide for her pleasures and her magnificence — he had seen her wear 20,000 louis' worth of jewels, while her husband had a perruque not worth thirty sous. She was proud and prone to take umbrage, but he had not crossed her. Indeed, she was very charming to him, showing him her display of shells: *'Une collection qui vaut quelques milliers de Louys.'* He had praised this, and bought some shells for himself, and she made him gifts of others, in exchange for which he was teaching her French. She was not fluent enough to agree with her husband that French should be spoken at supper, which placed Fletcher in an awkward position — he played the Carthusian, and stayed silent.

As for the third adult, Margaret, he described her as ugly, of good character, and possessed of £15,000 from her mother. He avoided her, having had an unfortunate experience in Hertfordshire, where his totally innocent attentions to a young lady had been misunderstood. He had wanted to improve his English, she had read too much into his kind of *'Galanterie'* — the English did not understand foreigners. So poor Peggy had to endure being shunned. As for the boys, their parents loved them with passion and were at that time terrified they might catch smallpox, again rife. They could not decide whether to stay in Town or go into the country. Fletcher hoped they would leave in a week or so. He was tired of London, and would be charmed to see another part of the country. Tern, he explained, was on the border of Wales, and he looked forward to bathing in the Severn. His image of an idyll may have been partly removed when he found that in close proximity to the Hall there was Tern Works, then run by ironmaster Joshua Gee — both he and the Works were a constant source of annoyance to Thomas Hill, and the lease (granted by Hill's father) was due to run until about 1760. Strangely, though, the colony of workers would be a foretaste of Fletcher's later life's work, as the 'Saint of Madeley'. On one of the journeys into Shropshire, possibly that first spring, he met a pious old woman who so impressed him that Mrs Hill told him to beware or they would be said to have a Methodist for a tutor — he had never heard of this strange new sect. Mrs Hill would have known about them, though, for her friends at Garth entertained them, and their daughter Sally was married to Charles Wesley.

We know little of the boys' education; one bill for school books survives: Fletcher was paid £1.7.6d for obtaining a Greek grammar, an Abridgement of Greek and Roman history, a dictionary, maps of Europe and the World, two French Common Prayer Books, and *Comus*. Two exercise books remain; and in one of his letters, written a few years later, Fletcher refers to reading *Telemachus* with his pupils. It would have been the basic classical fare, with a good share of grammar (to please their father) and a sound knowledge of French. The piety of their tutor must also have been noticeable, more as an eccentricity than an example. He accompanied the family in their moves between town and country, but in the country there were more distractions. Thomas Bell looked after the horses and took the boys setting and coursing, and their parents would have taken them on visits to friends and relations. There must often have been company at Tern. Sometimes the boys were cared for by Bell in their parents' absence: we have noted the visit to Llandrindod, and in the summer of 1754 the Hills spent time at Stamford with the Noels. The children probably felt closest to their mother, but their father also paid them what attention he could. In the autumn of 1751 his daughter Maria was ill, and he wrote to Dr Willmot: 'I thank you for yr care and kind endeavours for the life [of] my dear Daughter Molly whom I should ever greatly lament. When first I heard of her Ilness and that the fever continued after violent Bleeding at the nose I greatly feared mischeif . . . she had great strength of body as well as mind.' Some years later, when Sukey and the boys were recovering from measles, Hill's friend Bonnell wrote: 'I hope Miss Sukey and our Brother Walkers have quite Recovered . . . and that I shall live to see them dance a Merry Hornpipe next winter as well as to take a Turn with you in the Mall.' We can picture the two elderly gentlemen strolling and talking, with the four children, the girls watching the fashionable people, the boys more likely to have been interested in the horses.

Improvements at Tern continued, and in the winter of 1754 a new gardener was appointed — John Burkinshaw, who was to remain for nearly twenty years. Thomas Bell wrote to Hill on 23 December: 'Buckinger the Gardener was here yesterday and after walking Round the House and Garden he said the scituation was much better than he expected and that he never had seen any place where so great an Improvement was to be made at so small an Expence. As to a Bowling Green he says he will make you as compleat a one as any in England.' Capable Burkinshaw was never quite to Thomas Hill's taste; he found him too strong-minded. The following March, Bell could report: 'We go on with the Bowlingreen very well. The stone stepps and Dwarf Wall are taken away and what the Gardener calls a Bastian raised in the Place. The two Descents are Turff'd and the Angles on each side and the Front is designed for flowering shrubs and as the Green reaches nearer the River than the ends of the two walls there is an odd corner by the Hot-bed Garden Door which he likewise designs for Flowering shrubs.' Burkinshaw wanted the shrubs to be bought in London, as he considered they would be of better quality than those acquired in the country; and he wanted them by Easter week. He dictated his list to Bell who comments: 'I wish the shrubbs are spelt so as they may be understood for they have names that I am quite a stranger to.' The bowling green was for the boys' entertainment, and was ready, as Hill wanted, by the time they went to Tern that year. Gee gave up his lease early, and the Works were taken down in 1757. The following year Hill inherited the estate at Shenstone, and offered his wife the choice of houses. He preferred Shenstone, but she chose to stay at Tern, and to plan an extension to the front of the house. His mother's interest in the house and grounds, and her improvements, were to influence her son Noel, as we shall see.

Hill was anxious to advance his elder son, who was a favourite. Noel seems to have been devoted to his brother, to judge from an episode early in 1758. The older boy contracted smallpox, and there were wishes for his recovery from family and friends. His father wrote his thanks: Samuel was 'now I thank God so far recover'd as to remove from one Room to another and finds himself very strong and hearty; Noel continues well. he would not quit the

House; he would not have quit'd the same Room.' Then Noel caught the disease, and recovered. His father wrote to thank his cousin Richard Hill of Hawkstone (son of Sir Rowland): 'He behaved more refractoryly than his Brother and has clawed his face unmercifully.' Back at Tern that summer, Hill saw a chance to bring Sam to the notice of Lord Powis. On 26 July he wrote to his Lordship: he would have waited on him at Ludlow Races but 'agues are so very common I am advised to keep quiet for a few days to prevent a return this rainy weather. I proposed my son should have been the bearer of this but Mrs Hill thinks him too young by a year or two for the Races and such a full Assembly.' Sam was not yet fifteen. Instead Hill once more invited Powis to stay at Tern on his way back from Oakly Park to London. 'Mrs Hill promises you she will take the best care she can for your reception.'

Matters had taken a new turn with regard to the boys' education. Fletcher had indeed become an ardent 'Methodist'. He had been ordained by the Bishop of Hereford in 1757 and acted as curate to Hill's kinsman Rowland Chambre, at Madeley, but his enthusiasm and sermons had offended the local clergy. He had further upset his employer and his wife by the part he played in confirming their cousin Richard Hill in the same religious bent. Mrs Hill was afraid that he might influence Sam and Noel. So it was that they were sent to Cambridge in April 1759, though they were exceptionally young even for that time. Fletcher continued as tutor during their holidays but found their insolence and defiance impossible. Probably it was Sam who instigated the revolt. Fletcher and Mrs Hill were reconciled by the end of that year: he took his own room in London, but she pressed him to eat at Cleveland Court and to stay with the family, returning to Tern next summer. Before then, however, she was taken ill, and died on 14 February 1760, aged forty-one.

The previous day Thomas Hill wrote to Sam: 'your dear Mother's illness has prevented me writing to you and your brother sooner . . . I can't flatter myself or you with any pleasing hopes, I fear it would be in vain . . . it is the opinion of all your relations and friends here that you should not come to town and therefore I pray you to remain at College.' Fletcher wrote to Thomas Bell with the sad news. Bell replied 'I was in much fear that her case was dangerous from the time I had the first account of her Ilness . . . her Death is lamented here not only by her Acquaintance but by the poor and every one else that knew her character . . . I am sorry for the loss we all have but more particulary so for my Master and the young Gentlemen and Ladyes whose Grief must be Inexpressable.' Susanna Hill was buried at Atcham, in a vault under the chancel, on 26 February. Thomas Hill, once more widowed, had to take care of the children, now growing up.

Chapter 2
Sons and Heirs — Cambridge and After

Noel had just had his fourteenth birthday when he was admitted to St John's College, Cambridge, on 25 April 1759; Samuel was admitted on the same day. In May Noel received a letter from his father: 'I expressed in my letter yesterday to your brother the satisfaction it was to me to hear of your welfare at Cambridge and that you had passed your examination to the approbation of Dr Newcomb, Dr Brooke & Dr Pryce & I dont doubt but you will by a close application endeavour to merit the good character you have gained as a schollar, you will be directed by Mr Beadon in the course . . of your studies.' He suggested that Samuel should write to Dr Taylor to thank him for 'his very friendly civilities to you both'. John Taylor was Shrewsbury-born and St John's-educated, and the author of *Elements of Civil Law,* the subject of study chosen for both boys. Thomas Hill added that they should make themselves acquainted with 'two or three gentlemen of good character from Shrewsbury', and that they should read and speak French together.

The boys were admitted as fellow-commoners, the rank below noblemen; unlike the less wealthy undergraduates, the pensioners and sizars, the upper ranks could afford to be idle; and for those so inclined there were temptations enough — coffee-houses and taverns, women and horses, and drink. Samuel, at the age of sixteen had already succumbed to the last of these. A letter from a Mr Danvert to Thomas Hill in 1762 asks for his bills to be paid: 'forty fower Pound and upward which was for wines etc from allmost the first of his comen to collag till he left it to go a Brade.'

Sam did not stay the course, though he was given a degree through the influence of the Chancellor, the Duke of Newcastle, on his seventeenth birthday; it was a purely nominal mandate degree. In return, the Duke would ask for his vote for his candidate as High Steward, in 1764. A reference to Sam's going abroad is found in a letter from Howell Gwynne on 14 June 1760: 'as Mr Hill intends leaving England in a short time I am to wish him a happy Tour and a safe return.' Sam went to the Hague, where he had an introduction to the British Minister, Mr Yorke, but he did not have a happy tour. His father hoped that Sam would improve himself and make useful contacts so he wrote with advice, remembering his own early experiences and recalling the fame of Richard Hill: 'it was for the siege of Namur in 1695 that your uncle Hill gained such credit and at Hawkstone is a large picture of the siege, given him by King William', he reminded him as he suggested that Sam should visit Namur and the great university of Louvain.

Noel was to stay on at Cambridge, although his brother's experiences caused Thomas Hill to have misgivings. He wrote to Zachary Brooke on 6 October: 'I propose sending my youngest son again to College tho I have been often asked to what end and purpose unless to learn extravagance, vice and Idleness, & so become good for nothing.' He trusted that Brooke and Dr Beadon would look after him. Noel probably joined his father in London for the Christmas of 1760 (there is a reference to this in a letter of Thomas Bell) but it would have been a melancholy one, Mrs Hill having died that year, and Sam still abroad, giving cause for anxiety.

Next spring brought mixed blessings. Margaret Hill, now past thirty, was at last married — not for love, but for provision of an heir for the Earl of Harborough, formerly married to her stepmother's sister, Frances Noel. She was to have a son, in January 1767, but she died, and the child died a year later. Also in the spring of 1761 disquieting reports came from the Hague of Samuel's behaviour. His father begged him to refrain from drinking; he asked John Fletcher if he would accompany Samuel to Switzerland but the offer was turned down; he hinted at getting him some genteel employment. In May Samuel returned home. His father tried to get him a place at Court, Powis applying to Newcastle for a position in the new Queen's household (this was being arranged before the arrival of Charlotte of Mecklenburg-Strelitz in September). Powis wrote to the Duke on 12 July saying that the post of page might be suitable as the young man was only eighteen. After seeing Hill he wrote again, from Oakly Park, on 18 July, recommending Samuel as 'a good Scholar and a Master of Languages'. Hill wanted his son to be a Gentleman-Usher, which brought more money than a page. 'I wish your Grace could serve him!' wrote Powis. 'Few Commoners have a better Fortune than his Father.' Unfortunately, with the new reign, Newcastle's power was in decline — he was told that all the places had been filled.

That autumn brought more trouble. Fletcher wrote to Charles Wesley, from Madeley, in October, that he had had the mortification of seeing his former pupil at the Wakes there, completely drunk and boasting of his exploits at the Hague — a long debauch lasting 23 days. Sam's father did not know how to deal with his brutishness and godlessness. He was only just eighteen. Furthermore, Noel's elder sister Susanna, 'Sukey', was very ill at Tern. Maria and Mrs Noel, their grandmother, were there too. On 15 November Thomas Bell wrote to Hill in London: 'Miss Hill is now so weak that she can't suffer to be hove out of bed. Everyone about her thinks she can't live a week. She takes very little nourishment but has two composing drafts every night . . which cause her to sleap a great deale and makes the nights pass away easey.' She died quietly the next day and was buried as near her mother as possible.

Maria was ill with grief. Cheerful company was advised, perhaps a visit to Bristol. By January she was well enough to send for her boxes and drawing materials. By March she was much better; by summer she had a suitor. Sir Brian Broughton of Doddington Park near Nantwich was two years older than Maria; they were very fond of one another. The Noels and Margaret (Lady Harborough) encouraged her to accept him, and him to ask for £10,000 with her. This was the cause of contention, occasioning several letters from Thomas Hill's friend, James Bonnell, who had been asked to help. He predicted the consequences should the suit be left off: 'a Woman must look kindly upon none but her Woer, a Man may ramble all about the Town. a Woman must keep herself Chaste and be restless alone in her bed, a Man may have a bed fellow every night . . . when a match goes off it hurts a Woman a thousand times more than a Man — for Men cannot bear to think that the object of their Passion has ever had another man's mouth whispering in her ear.' If that happened it would cost £10,000 to get her married to another, and her friends would have been offended into the bargain. He also recommended the young man: 'Sir B— kept a Girl last Winter was twelvemonth but since this courtship has neglected all sorts of Women . . . I think it is a Good Sign, for a man of Cold Constitution is generally a peevish Husband.' At last Hill gave in and the wedding was announced on 2 September.

For Samuel a new possibility presented itself with the raising of the Shropshire Militia in October 1762. Thomas Bell paid Mr Bolas three guineas for his commission. A popular song commemorated Major Chase Price and his captains: 'Captain Hill has got knowledge by going abroad' — his drinking exploits would be well known as he boasted about them openly. The adjutant, Irwin, may have been with him at the Hague, and was not a good influence. Another captain, Edward Maurice, took him off to Montgomeryshire, out of harm's way, and sent a note with a present of grouse to say that 'Captain Hill is and has been in good Health since his arrival in Wales.'

Samuel took some interest in the house at Tern, left in its unfinished state since Mrs Hill's death. He decided to have the hall finished, complete with marble chimneypiece — he could then entertain his cronies to bumpers by a roaring fire after a day in the field. Noel continued at Cambridge: a series of college bills runs from December 1761 to March 1764. Payments were made for meals, tuition, books, and to the barber, glazier, smith, chandler, bedmaker, laundress, glover and hatter. His matriculation cost 4s 7d and his degree £4. After this he got a letter from his father — not of praise but of reproach. Sam was the favourite despite his faults; Noel got criticized whatever he did. 'I have repeatedly desired you to come to some resolution, and make Choise of some honourable profession most agreeable to yourself. if you should make choise of the Law, I would have you look out for Chambers . . . you have no time to loose.'

Without delay Noel got himself admitted to the Inner Temple, on 1 March 1763. Thomas Hill tried to appear more sanguine about affairs at home, writing in a draft letter dated 2 October (the recipient is not named): 'Our Shropshire Militia make a good appearance . . . Gentlemen and Ladys breakfast sometimes in the Camps, but no balls given as yet . . . as none of [Noel's] acquaintance here have heard from him they conclude he is at Newmarket.' Another, undated, draft to his son Sam expressed the hope 'for your happy Establishment, by marriage, with a person of proper alliance, fortune and fashion' as well as his fears of the 'vitious, drunken life you have abandoned yourself to'.

Mingling censure with appeal Thomas Hill refers to himself as an aged, chagrined, but still indulgent and tender father. The following August he was writing to a relation that 'our young Gentry have and are passing a Gay summer, assemblies and dancing sometimes 3 times a week, and sometimes 4, after a public Breakfast on the Bowling Green. My son is at Ludlow races, from thence to the Meeting of the 3 Choirs at Worcester.' Noel was by this time on his continental travels. In June 1764 he had received a letter from his father about his journey abroad: 'I wd advise you to see Holland . . I wd advise you set of immediately down the Maes from Liege to Rotterdam . . and to Utrecht.'

This was to be no Grand Tour! he was to take maps and grammars, and view fortified places; 'any officer will inform you by way of discourse how places are attacked and defended. inform yourself of the trade, manufacture method of agriculture of every place and of the Police of Brussels, Paris, Lisle and other places.' A dry programme indeed — a not so grand tour, unlike that of his friend Sir Watkin Williams Wynn a few years later. (Sir Watkin had

Maria Hill, Lady Broughton — sister of Noel Hill, by Francis Cotes. *(Courtauld Institute)*

no father to advise him.) He was in Paris in June 1768, visiting the sights, buying clothes, going to the theatre, taking lessons in fencing and dancing; in July he was going through Switzerland to Italy — by way of Turin, Milan, Como, Maggiore, to Florence and Rome. Sir Watkin became a connoisseur of art, and one of the Society of Dilettanti. He arrived in Naples in December, and Venice in January, where he bought two Titians; then back to Paris and home to Wynnstay for a grand coming of age.

The one bright interval in Noel's tour must have been when he joined Maria and Sir Brian for a visit to Spa and Paris. At the end of November there was another letter from his father. 'I have just received yours of the 23rd past that Sir Brian and your sister talked of returning to England in about a fortnight or 3 weeks, and that you shd return with them, except I should write in the meantime that I chuse you should stay abroad. I own to you I am perplexed what to answer. if you come home I fear you will lead the same indolent life you have done of late, unprofitable to yourself, and unless you frequent foreign company and enter into the spirit of improving yourself in knowledge of the world and learning and politeness you had better return home.' At least he had the regard of his sister and brother-in-law: Sir Brian left Noel £2000 in his will 'for the great Regard and Friendship I have for him and likewise whatever sum he may owe me at my decease.'

Maria was enjoying life as Lady Broughton. They had a fine house in Upper Brooke Street, entertained, and travelled to take the waters and partake of the pleasures of spas. One summer she wrote to her father from Tunbridge Wells. 'Time is so very scarce here that I can with great truth assure you that this is the first opportunity I have had since I left London [to write] . . I am stricktly forbid writing with the waters for fear of my head aching as it is apt to prove the consequence . . . I think I find benefit from these Waters notwithstanding the weather has been so dreadful bad that nobody has found the good from them that they used to experience; my apetite is very good and I am told I look a vast deal better than I did when I came here. There is a great deal of company here most very agreeable people . . . We are never at home here; it is a continual Round of Breakfasting Tea-drinking Raffling concerts Balls etc. You will say I must be better in health and spirits or I cou'd not bear such hurrys; but indeed every body here are so obliging and desirous of having us with them that it is impossible to avoid entering into all there partys.' She was writing in a bookseller's on the Walks, and friends were waiting for her to take a turn with them.

After his tour abroad we lose sight of Noel for some months, but in June 1765 he called on a neighbour in Cleveland Row and told him that he was going to Edinburgh to continue his studies. John Briscoe wrote to Thomas Hill that he was sure Noel's 'good Sence attended with a due application to that study . . will qualify him for one of the highest stations in life'. Noel wrote to his father on August 15, the day after his arrival in Edinburgh. He had that morning attended 'a very remarkable Tryal of a Lieutenant of the Army for committing Incest with his Brother's wife and giving her poison to give to her Husband which she effected, they were both condemned'. With that dramatic start he began a course of study with Hugh Blair, Regius

Professor of Rhetoric and Belles Lectures; Blair was celebrated for 'his literary style and social elegance'. On his way to Scotland Noel had met with other examples of social elegance, having a personal introduction to Lord Temple at Stowe, where he also met Temple's brother George Grenville. 'I heard a vast deal of Politicks', he wrote. Little wonder — the Grenvilles were a political force; their sister Hester was married to William Pitt, and there was much speculation that summer as to who would form the next administration. He also visited Chatsworth, the Duke of Bridgewater's canal, and Alnwick Castle where he dined with Lord Northumberland.

The year 1766 brought two deaths. Sir Brian Broughton died in January, and Maria was once again grief-stricken. In the same month Samuel Hill came to Tern alone. Bell wrote to Thomas Hill that his son had arrived 'quite coole and sober and talked very fairly and reasonably'. But on 14 February Bell wrote that he had been away from Tern a week and run up bills of nearly £350. Less than a month later Thomas Hill got an anonymous letter from Shrewsbury, informing him: 'your son is very much with Captain Irwin, who encourages him in, and procures for him, all that Indulgence which young men are but too apt to enjoy, in a soft Bed, and a soft bedfellow.' He was not to enjoy these pleasures for long. Within days he was back at Tern, needing the attention of doctors. Bell wrote afterwards: 'whether things might have been better or not had Mr Hill been advised and blooded the night before he had the falls I can't say, but it's agreed by all hands that it was too late when he came here for Physitians or Medicens to be of any service . . . neither would he give them a fair tryall.'

He was buried near his mother and sister on 27 March 1766; he was only twenty-two. Less than three weeks later Noel came of age. The only reference to this event is in the letter where Bell gave news of Sam's death. 'I wish him his health to enjoy his plentifull fortune and make no doubt but he will conduck himself agreable to the Expectations his friends have of him.'

A rough draft remains of a letter written to Noel by his father on 23 June 1766; he was evidently at Cambridge. 'I shall give you the best instructions in my power,' wrote Thomas Hill, 'to conduct yourself with the utmost sobriety and prudence — this would give you a good Character not only on your leaving the University but establish it on enquiry about you or otherwise in London, Bath, Tunbridge or wherever you may be. On leaving the College I would have you return your books and everything that belonged to yourself and your late Brother to London.' He was to take his leave, showing respect 'to all that Deserve it.' Mr Beadon would advise him 'how to manage property' and what to read. He should also enter himself at the Royal Society and the 'Arts and Sciences in the Strand'. There is a marked lack of affection and warmth, in contrast to the letters to the adored and profligate Sam.

Chapter 3
Heir to Tern:
Parliament and Marriage

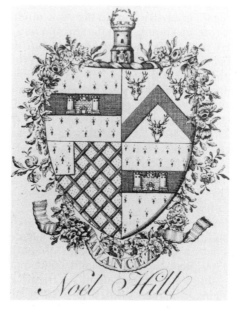

One of Noel Hill's bookplates, showing the arms of Hill, Harwood and Noel, with the Hill of Hawkstone motto. *(National Trust)*

As a younger son Noel Hill would have had to follow a profession, probably law, like his grandfather; his brother's death meant that he was now heir to an estate. There was one course, however, which he might have followed whatever the circumstances — standing for Parliament. His father's Shrewsbury seat was the obvious one for him. Thomas Hill was seventy-two when Samuel died, and there were two more years before the next election. As early as March 1767 Thomas Bell wrote to the elder Hill: 'Mr Hill is now talked of for the Borough in your Room and by all that I have heard about it is well approved of.' Thomas Hill's political world had changed much during the 1760s, ever since the accession of George III, who chose his former tutor Lord Bute as leader of the administration. The power of the Duke of Newcastle declined (we have seen how his application for positions in the new queen's household was ignored). An example which concerned Lord Powis, leader of Hill and other Shropshire M.P.s, is related in the Memoranda for 1759-1762 of the Duke of Devonshire, Newcastle's ally:

'January 1, 1761: When I came to Town, Lord Bute excused himself from having any concern in the promise the King had made to Lord Bath [to make him Lord Lieutenant of Shropshire, instead of Powis] . . he did not know [Powis] was my friend and that he wished anything could be done to satisfy Lord Powis. I said as to his being my friend that was a private consideration, the removing him a public one . . . and that Lord Powis had eight or ten members in the House of Commons, men of fortune that went with him. Whereas Lord Bath could not bring his own son into Parliament . . . that Powis and his friends were independent of all ministers and at all times ready to serve the King . . .'

Bute acknowledged the argument but the King kept his promise to Bath. Three Shropshire M.P.s — Bridgeman, Forester and Whitmore — went to the Duke of Devonshire to protest, but nothing could be done. Powis accepted Montgomeryshire instead, and was reappointed to Shropshire when Lord Bath died in 1764. The power once held by Powis and Newcastle was gone, but they both involved themselves in the 1768 election.

Since 1761 Hill's fellow M.P. for Shrewsbury had been Robert Clive. He had been made Lord Clive in 1760, through Newcastle, but it was only an Irish barony, not the English one Clive had wished for. His hopes of power lay in a Clive interest in Parliament: his father had been made member for Montgomery in 1759, his cousin George was given one of the Bishop's Castle seats, acquired when Clive bought Walcot Park for £92,000 in 1763, his friend John Walsh was M.P. for Worcester. Such an interest would be needed as his relations with the Directors of the East India Company worsened. He had acquired a fortune of about £300,000 when in Bengal, and been awarded a *jagir* of £27,000 a year by the Nawab. This award had troubled the Company; Laurence Sulivan, Clive's opponent, mentioned the matter in Despatches of March 1761. 'Colonel Clive's long illness preventing our having any conversation with him . . . upon the Nabob's grant to him of the annual rent of those lands now in our possession, which was paid before to the Nabob . . . we must therefore defer giving you our sentiments thereon.' Clive himself hoped that 'the receipt of the Jageer money for a few years will do great things.' As his opponents' power on the Board grew, he felt his fortune threatened. Trouble at home was averted when the situation in Bengal demanded his return there, in 1764. Before he sailed in June he sent notes from his home in Berkeley Square to Thomas and Noel Hill in Cleveland Court. He was sorry he would not have time to call, but thanked them for their friendship, and hoped for their continued support, if they thought it consistent with the interest of the Company (Thomas Hill was a stockholder).

In his absence, Clive's family and friends were busy on his behalf; his trustees included his wife, father, cousin and John Walsh. The death of Richard Lyster, one of the members for Shropshire, on 13 April 1766, offered an opportunity for a more prestigious seat than that for the borough, if the gentlemen of the county chose him. The trustees wrote to Thomas Wingfield (who was to be mayor in the crucial election year of 1768): 'As it is our

Intention to wait the Determination of the County Meeting before we take any steps with regard to the ensuing Election you will acquaint all Lord Clive's Friends therewith.' Another prominent Shrewsbury figure who worked on Clive's behalf was Dr William Adams, minister of St Chad's; he wrote on 2 May: 'The present object and only remaining hope of your Whig Friends is your Lordship's happy Return to head and unite the Interest.' Sir Henry Bridgeman, M.P. for Ludlow since 1748 on Lord Powis's interest, offered himself for the county without consulting his Lordship, which greatly offended him. But it was Charles Baldwyn of Aqualate who was chosen. The Clive camp still hoped he might be returned for the county at the 1768 election — as late as November 1767 Powis thought it likely — but Charles Baldwyn and Sir John Astley continued as county members, and Clive had to rely on his Shrewsbury seat. After his return in July 1767, 182 Gentlemen were 'invited to dine on Lord Clive's Trestle at the Talbot in Shrewsbury, Augt 3^d'; and Lord and Lady Clive were urged by Dr Adams to attend the races there early the following month, when a large company was expected.

Another matter concerned Clive in September: the East India Company were to discuss the matter of his *jagir*. Noel Hill wrote to his father that he had been to India House on the 22nd, where the pension was renewed for ten years. This satisfactory outcome must have given Clive confidence; the following year he appeared at the King of Denmark's Masked Ball, held at the Opera-house in Haymarket, as an Indian Nabob. Although no public declaration had been made that Noel was to succeed his father as M.P., Thomas Wingfield wrote, at the end of 1767, that 'it is understood by everybody at Shrewsbury that he will be a candidate and is often drunk to and wished success.' Wingfield thought that 'the old Gentleman at Tern means to trim matters', keeping in with Tories and Whigs alike. It was probably assumed that Noel Hill would be a mere tool of his father; in fact, although only twenty-two, he was to show confidence and independence during the campaign. Clive's ill-health had already driven him to Bath; his agents in Shrewsbury were Dr Adams and John Ashby — an eminent attorney who was later to manage some of Clive's estates. Wingfield could not actively support Clive because he was now mayor and returning officer; his promotion had been swift, and due to Clive. Another attorney, John Oliver, who did business for Thomas Hill, offered his services; his son, of the same name, also helped Noel — they were friends, and he was to be manager of Noel Hill's financial affairs for many years. The election was due in March, so a careful eye was kept on developments, and letters sent from Shrewsbury to Bath and London around Christmas 1767.

Wingfield wrote on 26 December to warn Clive of a 'Club' forming in opposition. 'I submit it to your Lordship whether you shou'ld not as early as may be engage Mr Noel Hill to unite his Interest heartily with yours and to declare this by applying joyntly to Mr Pulteney in town and by letter to Mr Mytton and others. I mention these two because they are spoken of as the Persons that have been thought of by this whimsical Party . . . Mr Noel Hill went to London this morning. I saw him yesterday and found him much impressed by the stories he had heard of this new club.' (In fact, Noel was to write with equanimity of the 'Club', in a letter to Clive.) Dr Adams' letter to

Clive is dated 29 December; it gives news of a 'new kind of Association that has been forming here among the lower Burgesses . . . They agreed to make a Fund for the relief of each other by putting something every week into a Box; and to act unanimously in everything in order to give them weight and consequence.' He believed that certain discontented people had 'infused Jealousies into others'. We have no testimony from any lower burgesses, but they may well have had grievances, as well as financial troubles from loss of trade that severe winter. On the other hand, Lord Powis dismissed the club with aristocratic hauteur: 'a set of Inconsiderable People, who despairing of any Contest for the Borough . . . have a Mind to do something to make themselves taken notice of, in order to get a little money dispers'd among them . . . Of this Class, there has always been at Elections there about fifty or sixty in Number, who have playd this Game.' Clive, however, was perturbed, not just because he was ill and nervous, but because the name of an old adversary had cropped up.

The Pulteney interest in Shropshire, formerly held by Lord Bath, then by his brother General Pulteney, had recently passed to the daughter of their cousin Daniel. Frances, the heiress, was married to William Johnstone — a Scottish advocate and opponent of Clive at East India House — who had now changed his name to Pulteney. Events were thus conspiring to threaten Clive's Shrewsbury seat. Taking Wingfield's advice, he wrote from Bath on 3 January to Thomas Hill. 'Sir, I have received Intelligence that a Club is formed in Opposition to the Corporation of Shrewsbury . . . an Encrease of this Association will most probably end in a Contest at the ensuing General Election, which besides the Trouble it would give the present Representatives, must unavoidably occasion a very great Expence.' He proposed the joint declaration which had been advised. It was Noel who replied on 5 January, trying to reassure Clive. 'My Lord, I have the honor of your's of the 3^d and shall be happy to unite myself with your Lordship as Candidate for Shrewsbury. I left that town last week, and thought it very quiet, notwithstanding I was well informed of the Club your Lordship mentions . . I understand from Mr George Clive you propose being in Town very soon, when I shall be glad to consult with your Lordship . . .' The letter is pleasingly free from the obsequiousness which characterizes many other letters to Clive. The Hills met Clive at his house in Berkeley Square on 14 January; he then wrote to Adams. 'The severe attack my health has lately suffer'd obliges me to leave England without Delay.' With a timely show of concern for the poor of Shrewsbury, he ordered Adams to disburse £200 on his account, on necessities. Then he left England, with his wife and friends, for a tour of several months; they took a villa at Montpellier. Noel set out for Shropshire.

He wrote from Shrewsbury to his father in London on 18 January. 'I got here about six o'clock yesterday evening, I rode from Tern as it is not quite safe to go in a Chaise over Atcham Bridge, part of it having fell in. there is to be a meeting in the Town Hall this morning about it.' The Quarter Sessions Orders for 3 February record that the bridge was damaged 'by the late Great Floods and Shoals of Ice' so that part of it had fallen and the whole would have to be re-built. On his first evening in Shrewsbury Noel took supper at Mr

The election jug of 1768, commemorating the occasion when Noel Hill was elected MP for Shrewsbury. *(National Trust)*

Kynaston's — his father's nephew, Roger Kynaston, who lived at 12 St John's Hill (his house was called Hardwick House); Adams and Ashby were also there. Thomas Hill's letter of resignation had been received that morning. Noel felt that Adams and Ashby were 'more attached to Lord C——e than any others here'. Indeed, his own supporters would have liked him to declare alone. The joint declaration was made, however, and Noel returned to London at the end of January, coming back to Shropshire at the beginning of March for the canvass. From the lists, it seemed that he and Clive would have a great majority. The 'neighbouring gentlemen' had been very obliging; Noel had the support of 'Mr Pygott', Mrs Lyster and Sir John Astley. But there was talk of Pulteney coming to the town to canvass. Noel had some rest by going to Longner, to the Burtons, to stay the night, but next day he went with John Oliver the younger to 'sollicit a Friend of his, for a Vote that was forgot', as the elder Oliver wrote to John Walsh. In Clive's absence, he was working hard at building support. Then he stayed with his cousins at Hawkstone, returning to Shrewsbury on the morning of 14 March. He called on George Clive, and also on Pulteney — this apparently displeased Thomas Hill (who did not want the Clives upset) but Noel stood his ground. 'I have conducted myself with the stricktest friendship to Lord Clive, I am sure Mr Clive ought to have acknowledged it to you; I shall continue still steady to their Interest, as we have advertised together, but I shall not be *persuaded* to act disrespectfully to Mr Pulteney.' He seems to have felt that he owed little to the Clives and would make up his own mind as to what was appropriate. At the poll, on 18 March, Noel Hill took most votes — 233; Clive had 149; Pulteney 97 — he petitioned against an undue election but withdrew on being offered two Scottish seats; he chose Cromarty.

The new Parliament met on 10 May, the Commons assembling in St Stephen's Chapel, their then home — it would not have held all the members if they had turned up. On the day they met there was a demonstration outside King's Bench prison, on behalf of John Wilkes: 'The riot act was read, and the soldiers ordered to fire', reported the *Gentleman's Magazine*. 'Several persons who were passing along the road at a distance, were unfortunately killed.' Expelled from Parliament in 1764, Wilkes had returned from France to be elected for Middlesex but it was illegal for an outlaw to be returned for Parliament. Henry Luttrell put forward a motion asking why the law had not been enforced; discussion was quashed by Lord North's adjournment motion, but the case would recur the following session. Clive returned to England in September, and paid for the entertainment of the burgesses of Shrewsbury, 'and as many other people as would come', as Bell wrote to Thomas Hill on 29 October. 'Four Houses were open but not so much Company as was expected I don't hear of anything that happened Extraordinary except that Captain Owen (with one arm) and another officer knockt up a Ryet in the Street but had the worst of the Battle in the end . . . Captain Fownes burst open Mrs Athertons door in order to get at her maid (as it is said) but she having people with her they gave him such a Dressing that he has not appeared since.' (Captain Owen was probably William Owen, a naval officer, who had lost his right arm at the taking of Pondicherry.)

The year 1768 brought an even more important event in Noel's life. We do not know how long the Hills had known the Vernon family of Hilton Park in Staffordshire, but as well as both families having houses in London, and the proximity of Hilton to Shenstone, there was a relationship through the Wentworth line between Lady Henrietta Vernon and Noel's mother. Lady Henrietta was the widow of Henry Vernon of Hilton; her title came from her own family — she was the youngest daughter of the Earl of Strafford. We learn something of family events in 1768 from Lady Mary Coke whose *Journal* was addressed to her sister Anne Lady Strafford, sister-in-law of Lady Henrietta Vernon. On 19 May she wrote that their niece Anne Vernon, eldest of Lady Henrietta's five daughters, was to marry Noel Hill; his father had a good estate, she wrote, but did not approve of the match. This suggests that once the parliamentary business had been settled satisfactorily Noel turned his attention to his personal wishes, and was not deterred by his father's opposition. His sister Maria had also met with difficulties, we may recall. As in that case their father's reluctance cannot have been on the grounds of family but of fortune, which Anne Vernon lacked. The match, like Maria's, must have been one of mutual affection. Anne was the second daughter to marry, her younger sister Henrietta having become the wife of Richard Lord Grosvenor in 1764. In September Lady Mary Coke had further news of the Vernons. She and Lady Henrietta, or Harriot as she calls her, were in the household of Princess Amelia, aunt of the King; Lady Harriet had already asked the Queen to take one of her daughters into her service. Lady Mary wrote: 'Lady Harriot Vernon's third daughter is appointed Maid of Honour . . . All on the sudden Her Majesty sent word she wou'd take Miss Varnon.' Lady Harriet requested that the honour might be done to Caroline as Anne 'had received a very advantageous proposal of marriage. This request was comply'd with, and her Daughter was at the Queen's Ball. What a great World to come into at once!' (Carry Vernon had not yet 'come out'.)

Noel and Anne were married on 18 November in London. Noel had written to Thomas Bell, hoping to have the new drawing room (part of his mother's extension to the house) finished, but it could not be done in time. So it was to the old house at Tern that Noel and Anne went after their wedding. This house, and the one in Cleveland Court, were assigned to him on his marriage; his father moved to smaller houses, in Abbey Foregate, Shrewsbury, and Thatched House Court, St James's. At Tern the couple received well-wishers and friends, and Noel's sister Maria was expected. Anne's sister Jane would also become a frequent visitor to Tern. (Their sister Lucy was subject to fits and may have been epileptic.) Their eldest brother, Henry, may already have been a friend of Noel's — they certainly shared a passion for hunting, and must have hunted similar country in Staffordshire. Henry Vernon also appears in a list of possible members of the Shrewsbury Hunt in 1769 — the main founder was Noel, who had been preparing for two or three years to get the hunt established. So it may have been through her brother that Anne came to know Noel Hill.

At the time of their marriage Henry was a lieutenant in the Royal Horse Guards, the Blues, which he joined as cornet in 1764. He enjoyed long periods of leave, including the last three months of 1768 and the first ten weeks of 1769. The returns for 1770 are missing, and his name does not appear in 1771; in 1769 he came of age. Noel and Anne Hill were often to visit Hilton, which is described in Pitt's *Topographical History of Staffordshire* as 'a large structure of brick and stone . . . built in the year 1700'. It was thus contemporary with Tern, but rather grander. 'It is surrounded by a moat, and the communication to this mansion is by a handsome bridge, which leads to the principal entrance. The park is very pleasant and secluded, abounding with all the varieties of sylvan and picturesque beauty displayed by groves, clumps and plantations . . . the plantations are chiefly of oak, and elm, which flourish in the utmost luxuriance.' We also have a description of Vernon, as remembered by 'Nimrod' — C J Apperley (who would have known him as the uncle of two contemporaries at Rugby School, William and Richard Hill). He wrote of 'the celebrated Mr Vernon — commonly called Harry Vernon — of Hilton, Staffordshire, the great dandy of the last century, and perhaps it is enough to say, he wore ear-rings. Notwithstanding this, he could ride to hounds, and was an accomplished sportsman — and particularly if you believed all he told you.' Noel Hill shared his brother-in-law's passion for hunting and horses, as well as for racing, but he could not compete with the Vernon dedication to the turf (nor their brother-in-law Grosvenor's). The Vernons' uncle, Richard Vernon, was so devoted to the sport that he lived at Newmarket where he bred horses and grew peaches.

We have an indirect picture of Anne Hill in a letter she received at Tern from her former lady's maid, Anne Sindefield, a reply to her letters. It offers a rare glimpse of a friendly relationship between mistress and maid.

'Dear Madam, I had the happiness to receive both your kind letters and am much obliged to you for your good advice which I shall allways be glad to follow in regard of the Ladays which I offered myself too it is very difecoult for me to say if the might a proved of me or not for it is hard to know Ladys tempers however I know I must submit so long as I am a Sirvant I am very much obliged to you Dear Madam for my charracter and every think that I have ever received from you . . . I am only sorry to hear you had enney uneasyness on my account as I heare you had . . . Madam I am sensible of the happiness I allways had in your sirvis . . . I am in know want for my Wages at present . . . Latt me be ware I will I shall never forgett that wonce Dear Miss Vernon . . . I am quite happy to heare that the Country has added to your Health and spirits . . . I will give you my word you shall never find me to tell lyes on eney Excount concurning the familay no it as allways been a fault in me to speke my mind too hoppen two the person face Lady Grosvenor was brought to Bed of a Son last Wednesay [of Lady Grosvenor's four sons, only one survived infancy — Robert, born in 1767] and is as well as can be expected you may be assured I will not show your letter I am quite happy you think I spell better I long to see you Dear Madam and hope you will not stay much longer in the Country . . . .'

It is also worth remarking that this letter was kept, when so many letters have been lost.

The once dear Miss Vernon, now Mrs Hill, having had her Christmas honeymoon at her new home, accompanied her husband to Town in time for some important business before the House of Commons. Wilkes's outlawry had been rescinded but he had been sentenced to twenty-two months in prison; he announced that he would petition for redress. In December he had had published, in the Saint James's Chronicle, a letter written in April 1768 by Secretary of State Weymouth, advocating the use of troops in riot control; the 'horrid massacre' was said to have been planned by the ministry. There were moves to expel Wilkes from the House, but some of the lawyers in the Commons held that he should be present. When the House reassembled after the Christmas recess, the mood was hostile to Wilkes. Lord North moved to restrict consideration of his case to points which would not necessitate general debate — some of the lawyer members dissented. The motion of 27 January was carried 278 to 131; Noel Hill voted with the opposition. When the repeated elections for Middlesex and the expulsions of Wilkes were debated, from February to May, he voted with the administration. Burke and North confronted each other in the debates; North appealed 'let not liberty be established upon the ruin of law.' As a student of law, Noel would have seen the force of the argument. Meanwhile, at Tern, Thomas Bell was worried about finances. He wrote to Thomas Hill: 'the Michaelmas Rents are now coming in and I have Received money lately and shall receive a Good Deale more this and the next Week but have paid a great Deale of money on Mr Hills account in Tradesmens Bills for Housekeeping Dales [deal?] and other materials for Building Workmens Wages etc. and all out of your money and as the demands on the Building affair will daily Increase and no more money on his account to be had of the tenants 'till near Michaelmas you and he must contrive your matters so that money must be had here to discharge the

Building Demands for this summer. I here he will be in the country the begining of May I will have his account made up by that time that [he] may se[e] how his affairs stand.'

The fact was that Thomas Hill, fond of making money but not of spending it, had passed on to his son the two large houses, but insufficient income. It is also clear from Bell's letter that Noel was setting about completing the improvements to the house begun by his mother. An undated note from Noel to his father must have been written when he returned to Tern that May; he sent it by Bell's hand to Abbey Foregate. 'Dear Sir, As you have frequently desired me to state clearly how our Account stands, and in our frequent conversations on that subject a Dispute has generally arisen between us, and my temper being warm I have sometimes made use of hot expressions, which I am always sorry for afterwards; I think it better to state the matter in writing. You may remember that on my marriage you agreed to give me Four thousand pounds to furnish the houses at Tern and Cleveland Court and to furnish other necessaries which indeed were wanting of all kinds.' He had been given only £2,700; he also pointed out that it was usual for a son on marriage to have the previous year's rents — those rents referred to by Bell, which were coming in only during the spring. A list of rents for Noel for 1769 amount to £1,900. From a later letter we learn that he had more than normal furnishing to do at Tern — there were extensive repairs to be done. 'The only Room finished in the new Building at Tern was oblig'd to be pulled to peices again owing to the Blunder of an Architect [Thomas Farnolls Pritchard] who built the Windows so high from the Ground that no one sitting could look out of them. I was advised and I think you approved it to alter the Windows round the House before I finished the other Rooms.' The advice came from Robert Mylne, but the work was re-done by Pritchard.

Early in June Maria wrote to her father from London: 'Pray Sir when do my Brother and Sister propose being in London? . . my situation in Town is so delightful that I do not intend leaving it very soon. I was at H. Court a few Days ago and stayed two nights but I cannot say it look'd so like the Country as the Lawn before my House here.' It was over three years since she had been widowed, with generous provision in Sir Brian's will: the house in Upper Brooke Street, jewels, plate and furniture, three carriages and all the horses, both Hampshire estates for her own use or the produce of the Lincolnshire estates and whatever sum was needed to complete a purchase in Hampshire, and whatever money was in the Funds for her use. Sir Brian's brother Thomas contested the will but she wrote confidently to him: she had taken Counsel's opinion, and asked Noel's advice. Although compelled to borrow temporarily from her father to complete the purchase, she won her case eventually, as a letter of James Bonnell's in 1773 shows: 'it would have been a shame to have lessened the substance of a Lady of such Spirit as hath added to the beauty of Green Park, and the environs of the King's Palace by a fine edifice.' (This house was at Stable Yard, St. James's.) In the summer of 1769 she had another suitor. Henry Errington was not obliged to haggle, as Sir Brian and Bonnell had done. He wrote to her father on 17 July: 'Mr Noel Hill having been so obliging as to write to acquaint you of my having had the honour to propose an alliance with Lady Broughton, I take the liberty to address you . . .' Lady Grosvenor invited Thomas Hill to Lower Seymour Street to meet Mr and Mrs Hill and Lady Broughton and Mr Errington. He and Maria were married by special licence in August. She retained the name Lady Broughton. Noel wrote to his father on 5 August: 'My sister was this evening married at her own house to Mr Errington, they went afterwards to Hampton Court . . . I hope they will be very happy.'

The Hills had a particular reason for returning early to London in 1769 — they were expecting the birth of their first child. Noel wrote to his father on 17 August: 'My wife thank God goes on very well and takes proper care of herself; I shall be in Shropshire the latter end of the month, and shall return I hope just in good time.' The business that took him to Tern was the work on the house, progressing well by this time: 'I think whoever dislikes the alterations now at Tern will alter their opinion when they are finished, at least they will please those that are to live in the House which is the chief matter.' He was also planning to landscape the grounds, employing the designer Thomas Leggett, who made his first visit to Tern that August. He was there again for brief visits in September, November and January — in the latter months the Hills were there too, with their baby daughter. Thomas Hill had replied to the news of her birth, on 7 October: 'I wish you both all happiness of a fine daughter.' He was glad they were all well, and offered to stand as godfather to the child. She was named Henrietta Maria, after her grandmother and two aunts. Their second Christmas together, with the addition of a baby, should have been a very happy time for Noel and Anne Hill, but there were hints of a looming family scandal. On 26 December Noel wrote to his father in London. 'I did intend to have been in town by the meeting of Parliament, had busyness that concerned the Public certainly come on, which I meant to write to know your opinion of, but now I must beg leave to consult you on another Subject tho' I firmly believe Lady G——r to be intirely Innocent, yet I know the world will be strongly prejudiced against her, so much so that I do not think it quite prudent that my wife should be in town, where affection for her sister would tempt her constantly to be with her, and should things turn out unfavourable for Lady G——r (tho' I have very good reason to think they will not) it might be more difficult for me to prevent my Wife going out thereafter in publick with her, than if she remains in the Country . . . my wife's spirits being extreamly low I am obliged to be constantly with her.' Her husband's affectionate care must have been a help, but Anne was fond of her sister Henrietta and wanted to be with her. It would seem that she wrote to her father-in-law, but she received a stern response: 'the voice of the Town in General and of your best friends . . . pronounce it as a very lucky circumstance that you are at such a distance at present . . . your own honour and that of your family should be no less dear to you than that of your husband and his family.'

The Town in General, with its love of scandal, must have been buzzing with stories of Henrietta's affair, for her lover was Henry, Duke of Cumberland, younger brother of the King. Her husband, Richard Grosvenor, was notorious as a rake, but that did not excuse his Lady; moreover, he saw the chance to cash in on the infidelity of his wife by suing his fellow Jockey Club member for damages. It was a raffish and unsavoury society that Henrietta

Lady Henrietta Grosvenor, sister of Anne Hill, by Gainsborough. *(National Trust)*

had found herself in since her marriage. Her portrait, done by Gainsborough a few years before, shows a pretty young woman with the enigmatic smile that his portraits of that period share. Horace Walpole did not name the 'lady of rank' but described her as 'a young woman of quality, whom a good person, moderate beauty, no understanding, and excessive vanity had rendered too accessible to the attentions of a Prince of the Blood.' He censured the Prince as a 'weak and debauched boy', who 'had been locked up with his brother, the Duke of Gloucester, till the age of twenty-one, and thence he had sallied into a life of brothels and drunkenness.' We cannot wonder at Noel's reluctance for Anne to be seen publicly with her sister, though they continued to see and help her privately. The intrigue had been going on for much of 1769, as was revealed at the later trial. The defence that Grosvenor had been the first to violate the rights of marriage, with a string of ladies confirming the claim, went for little, unless to persuade the jury to reduce the damages from £100,000 to £10,000. Mr Wedderburn outlined the case against, before Lord Chief Justice Mansfield, in July 1770. 'He set forth that his R.H. in his excursions to Towcester, in Northamptonshire, Coventry, Marford Hill, Whitchurch in Shropshire, Chester and St Alban's [places on the route from London to Eaton Hall] in order to meet Lady G——r, assumed, at different times, the names of Squire Morgan, Squire Jones, the Farmer etc. that he sometimes appeared as a young squire disordered in his senses and used to be called at the inns the Fool, particularly at Whitchurch.' (It sounds as if a fashionable masquerade had been taken too far.) The 'Squire's' servant, 'Trusty' — in fact his porter — had chalked a mark on the Prince's room at the inns, so that the lady could find it easily when choosing her own. Sarah Richardson, of the Red Lion at Whitchurch, testified that she heard rustling of clothes and opening of doors in the night, and found 'she did not know how many pins in the young man's bed'. The suspicious husband had his wife's letters intercepted and in December sent his butler and groom to the White Hart in St Alban's. They broke in on the couple. Her ladyship said, 'I suppose you have done a very fine thing now'; the butler said he was sorry. The Duke had fled into the next room and said, 'Take notice I am not in Lady G's room', to which the butler replied, 'no you are not now but you was this minute'. When they knew who he was they let him go.

Miss Vernon — another of Anne Hill's sisters, possibly Caroline. *(Courtauld Institute)*

This was when the disquieting rumours reached Tern, causing concern to Noel and grief to Anne Hill. Another of her sisters was equally concerned, but with rather different feelings. Caroline, as Lady-in-Waiting to the Queen, was very anxious because the Queen and the Princess of Wales had heard her 'censured in this curs'd affair'. At the time of its report on the trial, the *Gentleman's Magazine* published a letter said to have been written by Caroline to Henrietta on 15 December. 'I am wretched to find that a passion for a certain person wrongly intitled to it has so much got the better of you that the loss of your own reputation, *of mine,* and of both our happinesses are to you of no consquence . . . you must be banished from all your Relations'. She warned her older sister that Mr Hill would 'not suffer his wife to be seen in your Company . . . and as to myself, Mama will take care to keep me from ever having a sight of you.' This must have been a bitter disappointment to the already afflicted Henrietta, but she retained the support of Noel and Anne, as of Mama — Lady Harriet — and probably of her other sisters. Hilton offered a welcome refuge, but she eventually went back to London, late in 1771, to a house in Cavendish Square. Some of the scandalmongers still criticized her, but she was freed from an unhappy marriage, and the following year her husband settled £1,200 a year on her. (When he died, in 1802, she immediately married General George Porter, at Shoreham; he became Baron de Hochepied.) The Prince, who had so cravenly rushed to another room when discovered, straight away abandoned Lady G. for a rich merchant's wife, before moving on to Mrs Horton. He committed the graver sin of marrying her, and contributed to the passing of the Royal Marriages Act of 1772, which was much debated in the Commons.

Chapter 4
Country Pursuits

For those with houses in both Town and Country (the former often rented), the London season occupied winter and spring, when Parliament met. At the end of the session, in May, country gentlemen returned to their estates. Noel Hill was in London for part of the spring session of 1770; in May his footman, William Bennett, prepared for their journey back to Tern. He had the travelling trunks repaired, his master's frockcoat cleaned and his silk stockings washed; he paid the subscription to the *Sporting Calendar,* posted letters and bought stationery; he also bought powder, pomatum, a razor strap, a shaving box with soap, and a toothbrush. The journey, via Barnet, St Alban's, Dunstable, Four Crosses and Ivetsey Bank, involved payments to drivers, ostlers and bootcatchers at the inns, and for post horses and turnpikes, for the post coach and phaeton. Once in the country, Noel could turn his attention to his family and friends, to the social round, and to plans for the house and grounds.

Hilton Hall, Staffordshire, home of the Vernon family. *(William Salt Library)*

Work was carried on at Tern from 1770 to 1774 by the garden designer Thomas Leggett. Leggett had worked at Eaton in the 1760s, the estate of Hill's brother-in-law, Grosvenor, and also at Chirk. He visited Tern in May, June, July, September and October 1770 — he was also working at Wynnstay at the time. Sunken fences were dug and planted with quickthorn; they ran from the upper corner of the intended orchard to opposite the island, and from the paddock wall by the dog kennels, curving round the green, down to the river Tern. The slope from the house to the river was lowered and the river widened. Gravel paths were flanked with turf, and hay and clover sown beyond the pleasure gardens. Tree planting was extensive. Hill's gardener, John Burkinshaw, acted as Leggett's foreman from June to November 1770, earning sixteen shillings a week instead of his usual nine. Noel had visited many fine places, a popular diversion for the Georgian gentry who could study and admire, if not emulate, Stowe and Chatsworth. On a more modest scale there was Hilton with its sylvan attractiveness. Noel's brother-in-law, Henry, may have been engaged in similar plans at the same time; having left his regiment he could give more time to his estate. The *Topographical History,* which describes Hilton, records: 'The late Mr Vernon was an early planter, and lived to see some of his first efforts fast approach maturity.' They often visited each other, and must have shared ideas. They were both at Tern with Leggett in March 1774, viewing the work of the past few years. Large numbers of oaks, hornbeams, beeches and chestnuts were planted, and limes, balsoms, almonds, cherries, walnuts, weeping willows, striped sycamores, junipers, cypresses, Scots pines, firs and larches.

Tern Hall, c. 1775, home of the Hill family, after alterations. *(National Trust)*

The house at Tern had been put right, and the rooms planned by Noel's mother were completed. Chimney pieces for the upper chambers and dressing rooms were commissioned, through Pritchard, from the carvers Nelson, van der Hagen, Swift and Abraham. Hill was not satisfied with Pritchard, who had made the blunder over the windows, and was consulting the London architect Robert Mylne, who had several Shropshire clients at this time. One of these was John Mytton of Halston, the Master Mytton who went to school at Fulham; Mylne had been visiting Halston since 1766. In the same year he began advising on alterations at Condover, for Miss Leighton, daughter of Mytton's cousin. He began advising Noel Hill in 1769, among other things ordering a chimney piece from John Deval. Miss Leighton's brother, Charlton, Noel's friend, had been travelling in France and in Italy after leaving Cambridge; on his return to England he took over Loton Park, by agreement with his father, Sir Charlton, who lived elsewhere, on an allowance. Mylne went to Loton in January 1773 and was asked for designs for altering and improving Loton Hall, and for a sketch of the plantation. This must have been when the changes at Loton were begun — the villagers of Alberbury were moved to Wattlesborough Heath. Two days after his visit to Loton, Mylne was at Tern. Back in London he worked on his drawings, including those for Hill. 'Sent Mr Hill at List of Alterations and amendments recomended to be made to his house at Tern, in its present state.' He must have seen Hill in person in March, for the Diary entry reads: 'Gave Mr Hill a Plan, Elevation and Section of a large set of Stables etc. A Design of 3 Plans of an Elevation of a Gardeners House. A Plan and Elevation of a Green house. A Method with directions for fitting up the Saloon for Books, Billiards etc.' In May he sent further plans and washed drawings; and he waited on him at the end of August with a sketch for a lodge. In 1774 he made further visits.

The Hills continued to visit socially, friends and relations, as we see from turnpike payments in Bennett's accounts. In August 1770 William Bennett had been promoted from footman to butler; his wages were doubled, to £20 a year, with 2 guineas tea allowance. He accompanied Hill on both social and business occasions. On the visiting list was Hilton, Loton Park, Hawkstone and Longner (sadly, Ann Burton, last surviving child of Thomas Hill's first marriage, died in 1771). They went to Tatton (there was a family connection with the Egertons) and to Acton Burnell (another connection — Sir Edward Smythe's brother Walter was married to Mary Errington, sister of Lady Broughton's husband). People also met at public events: militia balls, races and hunts, the theatre, and various clubs. Sir Uvedale Corbett's Club had been founded in 1684 as a Whig club; in 1770 Noel Hill presided and bought madeira for the meeting. In August that year three days were spent at the Salop Assizes. Then there was a more pleasant social gathering: each summer they resorted to Longnor where the Caractacus meeting was held. This dated at least from the 1750s, as we see from an entry in the *Gentleman's Magazine* of 1755: on August 5 'The *Caractusian* society was held, according to annual custom, upon that memorable mount *Caer Caradoc . . .* which name was derived from *Caractacus*, that heroic *British* Prince, who made a noble resistance upon the summit of this hill, against *Ostorius . . .*' The practice may have begun as the whim of a learned clergyman, but it came to serve as yet another occasion for local gentlemen to meet. The original cold meal on top of the hill was, before long, abandoned in favour of dinner at the Bowling Green Inn. Robert Corbett recorded in his diary that on Tuesday 28 August 1770 the meeting was very large and genteel — there were seventy-seven pëople and Noel Hill presided.

A few weeks later came the Shrewsbury Races, held from 18 to 20 September. A £50 purse was given by Lord Clive and Noel Hill, the M.P.s, and it was at this meeting that the first sweepstake at Shrewsbury was planned for the following year. The eight subscribers each gave twenty-five guineas. Of these, Lords Powis and Clive were interested in political advantage; the others were keen followers of the sport. Robert Pigott, a member of the Jockey Club, was known as 'Shark' at Newmarket. He once backed his father's life against that of a Mr Codrington's father, not knowing that Pigott senior had just died in Shropshire; refusing to pay, he was taken to court, where Lord Mansfield gave judgement against him. Edward Maurice of Lloran we have met before, as a captain in the Militia with Sam Hill. An active sportsman, he was described many years later by Richard Fenton as 'an old Cherokee Country Squire; affected to talk hard; carried a hunting pole; dress old costume. Gold Bobbin waistcoat and gold lined front; 3 or 4 terriers. Talked of the best days of the Druid Society.' Sir Watkin Williams Wynn was the youngest, having come of age only the previous April. The other three subscribers were Lord Grosvenor, Henry Vernon and Noel Hill — all brothers-in-law. The recent court case over Henrietta was clearly not allowed to stand in the way of serious sporting business. One of the horses entered was Grosvenor's chestnut colt, by Match'em. This stallion was in the class of Eclipse and Gimcrack: in 1771 they were at stud, Eclipse at Epsom and Gimcrack at Newmarket, both at 25 guineas a mare; Match'em stood at Catterick Bridge, at 20 guineas. (True to his breeding, the chestnut colt, Examiner, was to win the first Shrewsbury sweepstake.) The Clerk of the Course at Shrewsbury was Edmund Littlehales, listed in the 1768 poll book as a draper, of Mardol Head. After the Shrewsbury meeting Noel went with Vernon to Hilton; they both attended the races at Lichfield but Noel left for home before the end of the meeting — the birth of his second child was due soon. The Hills' first son was born at Tern on 21 October 1770, the only child of theirs not born in London. He was named Thomas Noel, after his grandfathers. Turnpike payments suggest that the servants who took the news to Hilton escorted Lady Grosvenor back to visit her sister, of whom she was very fond.

The last race meeting of the year in this part of the country was at Holywell in Flintshire — matches and races originally run on Halkin Mountain by horses belonging to members of the Holywell Hunt. Some of the members are familiar names: Mr Vernon, whose bay mare Boadicea ran in 1768; Mr Hill, whose black gelding Clown ran the same year; Mr Maurice, whose black colt Guinea-pig (by Lord Grosvenor's Arabian) won the following year. In the Gold Cup of 1769 Mr Maurice rode Sir Watkin Williams Wynn's winning horse Brown George; Vernon rode his own horse Willow into second place. *Adams' Weekly Courier* reported on 14 November 1769: 'There were the greatest number of Noblemen and Gentlemen at the Holywell Hunt Races

Noel Hill's horse, Bishop. *(Courtauld Institute)*

that ever was known, who made a most brilliant appearance, and at night there was a Grand ball given by the Gentlemen Subscribers to the Holywell Hunt.' The meeting of 1770 was run over the 'new course' — Hill's horse Bishop was ridden in the Gold Cup by Mr Bell Lloyd (who, as a member of the Grosvenor Hunt, is depicted in Stubbs' famous painting). Hill stayed on for the hunt; he was accompanied by William Bennett, and by his coachmen, grooms, gamekeeper, and keepers of dogs and horses. These are named in the accounts: Trubshaw Stiles, John Harris, Hugh Stedman, Humphrey Kirklands, Henry Evans, Harry Warren and John Staunton. It was a considerable undertaking to go over to Holywell and Noel Hill gave up this hunt after the 1770 season. There were other hunts closer to home, particularly the Shrewsbury Hunt, of which Hill was a founding member and prime instigator; he was president in 1769, its first year. A letter he wrote to Nicholas Smyth, at Condover, early in January 1768 shows that he had been making great efforts to acquire hounds. A Mr Ascham was proposing to part with his pack and Hill hoped to acquire 'about Ten or Fifteen Couple of Welps, fit to enter; five Couple of steady Hounds, and his young Stallion, for which I would willingly give him his price . . . as I am partial to his Hounds, and very desirous of establishing our Hunt by having a good pack at once.' He asked Smyth's opinion, 'and what Plan you think would be most Conducive to make our Pack as good in one Twelvemonth as Our *Neighbour's* which has been his whole study for five years. I own it would please me much to see Ours flourish next Year . . .'

The next year the Shrewsbury Hunt was established. A declaration dated 16 June 1769 reads:

'We whose Names are hereunto subscribed (Being Members of the Shrewsbury Hunt) do hereby agree to meet and dine at the Coffee house on the third Tuesday in every Month, and that an Ordinary shall be provided for Twelve Members certain at Two Shillings Sixpence each, And that every Member pays his Ordinary whether absent or present, And that every Member be permitted to bring one Friend . . . that the Half Crowns paid by the absent Members shall go to the stock purse, and that every Member subscribes one Guinea annually to support any accidental expences And Mr John Oliver is appointed Treasurer to receive the same. That no one be admitted a Member of the Society but by Ballatt except the Gentlemen whose Names have been delivered this day to Mr Hewett.'

The first names are Noel Hill, Nicholas Smyth and Edward Maurice. A long list of 'supposed members' includes Charlton Leighton who, although abroad, supported the project, Lord Grosvenor (perhaps the Neighbour to whom Hill had referred?), Sir Watkin Williams Wynn, several other Leightons, and Henry Vernon — all keen sportsmen, and some close friends. It seems that hunting wear was to consist of a blue frock coat and blue coat with gilt buttons engraved SH, white breeches and waistcoat; dress uniform might be worn for meetings instead. Originally two meetings were planned, but the spring meeting was dropped. In Hill's accounts we find regular payments to Alexander Hewitt of the Coffee House for the hunt kennels. These had been referred to in the letter to Smyth, showing that the preparations had been careful. 'If you advise buying all Ascham's Pack I will do it, for as our Chief Expences are now over for these Years having finish'd Our Kennel, and bought our Horses it will be Folly not to have a good Pack.' He signed himself 'Your very Sincere Friend'; several other members must also have been his friends, and we see Noel here in the role of leading spirit. Hill also supported other hunts, such as the Condover, in Smyth's corner of the county; Hill was president of that hunt in December 1773.

Glimpses of life in the country, some sporting, are given in Bennett's accounts. There are the expenses at races and hunts, a payment to the huntsmen of the Shrewsbury Harriers for a hare, to a man for bringing a greyhound from Sir Charlton Leighton's estate, Loton, 7/6d paid for a sheep killed by Hill's hounds. Other items have a more personal touch. 'Paid your Hair Dresser during the Militia meeting 4 times . . . to Silver you had of me the Ball night Hunt week . . . Paid for Lady Broughton's Picture 15/– . . . ribbon to tie your hair [this occurs frequently] . . . 1/– you had of me to give to a poor man, when going into the Infirmary . . . Master's birthday this week . . . Trubshaw Stiles, airing Miss Hill [young Harriet] . . . double box Shrewsbury cakes sent to Lady Harriet Vernon . . . Paid your Hairdresser this week NB dress't 3 times the Ball Day . . . 10/6d to a poor Old man, beyond Atcham, his name Thomas . . . to Christmas Carol singers . . . to Morris dancers 2/6d . . . to Mr Preist etc playing country dances . . . paid to woman at Atcham for schooling of 2 poor children 4/– . . . to Sir Charlton's man the Fee for half a doe 5/– . . . the Musick Fishing party £1.1.0 . . . Play tickets . . . Xmas box to a little boy that you keeps to School 2/6d . . . Mr Vernons servant . . . 12/– to Burkinshaw for 18lb honey, sent to Miss Vernon . . . fiddlers playing to servants . . . music for servants' ball 10/6.' The ball for the servants, in the new year, came at the end of the country season.

Thomas Hill did not approve of Noel spending his money on hunting and other frivolities. When Anne Hill wrote to her father-in-law on 3 December 1770, telling him that his little grandson was well 'and thrives surprisingly', she also told him that Noel had resolved to quit the Holywell Hunt. The main purpose of the letter was 'to sollicit for an additional income as we must otherwise be obliged to trouble you by renewing our application every year for money, as Mr Hill has consulted all the wisest and most prudent and even penureous men in this country both of your Friends and his and they all agree that he cannot live upon his presant Income which imboldens me to write to you, but what I trouble you for cheifly at presant is to tell you that he is greatly distressed for two thousand pd, he very well remembers the one he had of you last which was to pay what he had exceeded of his Income and one of these he wants now is for the same purpose this year . . . the other thousand he wants is to pay for fitting up the old House here and many things he was oblig'd absolutely to do here as to mending and fitting up places which gave him no pleasure but was obliged to do them as nothing had been done here this fifty years, and in a few years more must have cost double the money.' Noel Hill's rent roll for the half year due Lady Day 1769 shows the estates he was given and the rents they brought in: Atcham and Tern £173.2s.8d; Boarton £100; Hampton Wood £50; Weston Lunningfields £88.5s.0; Yorton £23.52.0; Houldstone £10; Paynton £78.15s.0; Shenstone £362.14s.9d; tithes £69.6s.2d. The total for a year was thus less than two thousand pounds, and there was much upkeep. The plea can have brought no immediate result, for in February Noel had to make a statement of his affairs for his father. The family returned to London at the end of January, in the chaise and coach and six.

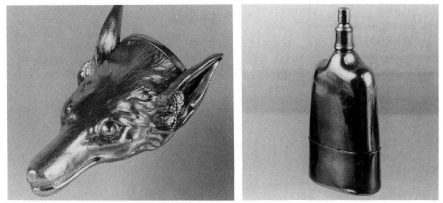

A silver gift fox head stirrup cup and silver flask, belonging to Noel Hill. *(National Trust)*

Anne Hill with her eldest son, Thomas Noel Hill. *(Courtauld Institute)*

On Friday 15 February Noel set about the statement of his finances; his letter to his father ran to seven pages. It is worth quoting in some detail:

'Dear Sir, I have been told within these two Days that you wish'd to have a State of my affairs and my Frequent Request for an Increase of Income put down in writing. This I with great Chearfullness got up this morning at seven o'clock to do . . . as I shall lay my affairs before you in the most open and Candid manner, and have not in the following

Requests asked any more than what will just enable me to keep my word that on an Increase of Income I should never apply to you again and not exceed it; so I hope you will be kind enough to give me a speedy and Favorable answer. My Requests and the State of my Circumstances follow.

The Remainder of the Entailed Estates to be given up to me the Rent Role of which amount to about the sum of   1500£ p.an. Brompton and Cronkhill to be also given up to me or any other of the unentailed Estates the Rent Role of which should amount to 500£ p.an. . . . when added to my present Rent Role . . make together   4000£ p.an. Which will not produce more than Three Thousand Pound neat money per annum. Ten Thousand Pounds to be lent on Mortgage on Brompton and Cronkhill or any other Estate given up to me of the Yearly value of Five Hundred Pounds without Interest for Five Years, and then to bear Interest at the Rate of Four Pounds per Cent . . . [He added later than if he did not live within his means his father could leave this mortgage to whom he pleased.] Having now been married upwards of two years my Rent Role being but just the Half of what I then did and now do request of you . . . You gave me on my marriage an Estate of Eleven Hundred and odd Pounds per an. but as I married in Novr you had not receiv'd the Mich^s Rents and did not till Lady Day. I could not consequently receive any rents till the next Nov^r . . . I may now venture to assert that the sum you gave me down at my Marriage to furnish every Necessary will fall short 3000£ The Reasons for which I shall presently explain.

Mr Probert assures me that a great sum of Money will be wanted to raise these Estates in the manner that will most benefit myself and Children hereafter . . . I remembered to have heard my Mother frequently say that you annually spent 3500£; Mr Bell and others have since assured me of the same. Before I married I was already Member for Shrewsbury, at the time of my marriage I found it your Choice to retire to a smaller House both in Town and Country and to place me in those Houses in which you had for so many years lived extreamly Handsomely . . I Sir felt an Ambition to Live in Equal Credit with my Neighbours and to act as justly by my Tradesmen . . . You know Sir that in the Country I live in the Neighbourhood of Gentlemen of large Fortunes who live Handsomely and in an Hospitable way, I need not tell you who lived so many years among them in at least an equal Style that I in my Situation must not live in a much Inferior one; on these Grounds I now with submission lay these Proposals before you.'

So, in lawyer-like manner, Noel argued his case, reminding his father of 'the Blunder of an Architect' who built the windows too high, so that the work had to be pulled to pieces — it was impossible to complete the work for the sum given him on his marriage. He then turned to the need to have money in hand, acknowledging former imprudence; he wanted money deposited at Child's to draw on. He may have received a necessary increase in income, but he was not to have money to hand, and had to borrow modest sums from various people, including his mother-in-law and Lucy Vernon. They probably sympathized with him on having such an economical father.

Noel and his wife were late coming to Tern in the summer of 1771. He wrote on 20 July to Thomas Hill: 'Mr Errington and Lady Broughton have desired my Wife and I to accompany them to Andover where they are going to settle some busyness in regard to their Hampshire Estate, we propose seeing Lord Pembroke's [Wilton] and some other Places in that Neighbourhood . . . My Wife and I with the Children who are very well, hope to be in Shropshire the first week in August.' He had paid brief visits to Tern in the interim to see to estate matters. His letter to his father contains the comment: 'Perhaps had they waited till this time the Meadow and the 3 Pieces might have produced more Hay, but I ordered them to begin early as I had a good deal of Hay Ground. I was afraid if they should have a Lingering Harvest it would be late in the season before they could get it in.' This would seem to be a response to a criticism by his father.

Among Thomas Hill's papers are rambling notes, possibly 'memoranda' of what he wanted to say or write. One such dates from 1771, and complains of the 'loss of time and fortune' caused by his son's hunting — a particular grievance of the old man, who did not care much for country pursuits. Noel Hill was acclaimed by Apperley, 'Nimrod', as one of those conspicuous in the hunting world, 'whose country extended from ten miles below Shrewsbury to Lutterworth in Leicestershire, a distance of upwards of seventy miles.' As we have seen he had his own kennels and gamekeeper, points which his father complained of. His friend and brother-in-law Vernon is the earliest person known to have hunted in the Shifnal area, according to Auden in his *Short History of the Albrighton*. Vernon far outdid Noel Hill in horse-racing, however: the *Sporting Calendar* for 1775 lists fifteen horses belonging to Henry Vernon; his uncle Richard Vernon had twice that number, including several by Herod and Match'em. At the Shrewsbury meeting in 1771 Vernon's bay colt Minister won a sweepstake on the last day. The matter of hunting remained a contentious one between Thomas Hill and his son, but Noel was not to be put off his sport, nor the improvements at Tern.

The seasonal routine was somewhat altered in the next two years by the births of another daughter, Anne, in London, on 30 May 1772, and another son, William, in 1773. On 24 August that year Noel wrote to his father: 'I have the pleasure to acquaint you that Mrs Hill was safely delivered of a very fine Healthy Boy between twelve and one o'clock this morning.' He had been assured that the child was 'as fine a one as ever seen', and Mrs Hill was as well as could be expected.

Noel himself, though, was suffering from an old bilious complaint, brought on by the hot weather. On 30 August he wrote that he would not be at the races in Shrewsbury as he wanted to wait until his wife was well enough to travel. During their protracted stay in Town that summer Thomas Hill kept them informed of events in the country (to judge from his memoranda). He was critical of the work going on at Tern: 'I was in hopes you had given orders to put a stop to the finishing your new Garden Wall but I find they are working with double hands of late.' He criticized Burkinshaw's tree-planting, and later offended the gardener by sending fruit to Tern! Then there were the workmen: 'Your new Carpenter who has no Character himself has recommend to you a stone cutter who was employed at both the Bridges but discharged both.' 'Legged, Lee and Scotholck have a fine time of it. They will be for ever projecting.' So we learn that Leggett, Richard Lee the master carpenter, and the builder Jonathan Scoltock were all at Tern. Lee and the Scoltocks had often been employed at Tern, and were to do much work there in future. Thomas Hill suggested economies: 'Crown Glass which cost dear not to be to offices' — the service rooms — especially where trees would hide them. He disapproved of the new windows: 'the old Transhome windows had a look more becoming.' He further complained of 'what Lee is doing [to] the old offices and stables.' It is very difficult to read the scribbling, especially when the old man's emotion rises: 'get rid of yr Dogs and horses, huntsmen, whiperin and such vermin in time and immediately.' We almost miss the short sentence of praise for James who is 'a good servant the children's fondness for him shows it.' James Wright was the under butler and often appears in Bennett's accounts, getting toys or a guinea pig or squirrel's cage for the children, bread for them to feed the deer in St James's Park, a book for little Harriet, or paying the blind fiddler to play for them at Tern. That summer the three children were looked after by nurses and servants there. Sometimes Bennett took them into Shrewsbury, probably to visit their grandfather.

There was also news of friends, and comments on election matters in which he would still like to have been involved. On 7 August Thomas Hill wrote that Thomas Bell had lapsed again; the old steward had been ill all that year. On 8 September some of their neighbours set off for the Worcester Music Meeting, a forerunner of the Three Choirs Festival. That year the beautiful Elizabeth Linley, wife of Richard Sheridan, sang there: she 'took leave of an admiring public in the full lustre of unrivalled talents', as the annalists of the festival recorded. Noel's friend Charlton Leighton had gone, 'in hopes of seeing Miss Vernon' — one of Anne's sisters, probably Jane. If this hints at an attachment there was no romantic ending; neither of them ever married. Mr Vernon's three horses also went past the house in Abbey Foregate, on their way to Shrewsbury Races. The colt True Blue won the sweepstake on the first day; the chestnut Ratoni came second in another race; the black gelding Venture won his race. Before Noel, Anne and young William came to Tern, Thomas Hill asked Mrs Bennett to have the house well aired — surely an unnecessary instruction. The journey was made in late September. The races were over, but the hunting season began: Leighton was president of the Shrewsbury that year, and Noel Hill president of the Condover Hunt early in December. That autumn Thomas Bell died, after nearly forty years' service to the Hill family. He was buried at Atcham on 11 November 1773. We learn little of his personal life from his letters; his will is the only other testimony. In April that year Noel Hill had written: 'I believe he has left most of his fortune amongst the Roman Catholicks of the Acton Burnell side of the country.'

There were many bequests to Bell's relations in Northumbria — Bells, Taylors, Youngs and Stokoes. Always compassionate, he left something to the poor of Atcham. Small sums were left to his friends and executors — Francis Bradshaw of Eshe near Durham, and Richard Cooper of Ruckley, Shropshire, to whom he also left his silver tobacco box. The main bequest was to 'my worthy friend Sir Edward Smyth [sic] of Acton Burnell . . . £500 to be paid by my executors in 12 months after my death.' This leads us to wonder about the connection with the Smythes, a leading Catholic family, who also originated in Northumbria. Edward, the first baronet, came from Eshe, county Durham, and married Mary Lee, heiress to Langley and Acton Burnell. It was during the lifetime of his son Richard that Bell became steward at Tern, in 1734. The connection of both men with Eshe suggests that it may have been through the Smythes that Bell came to Shropshire. The Sir Edward to whom the bequest was made was Richard's nephew. There was a strong Catholic group based in Acton Burnell, at a time when the faith was proscribed. Why did Bell make such a large bequest to the family? Was he grateful to them, or, as Noel Hill's remark suggests, was the money intended for the Catholic community? Until the Catholic Relief Act of 1778, bequests for the support of the Catholic religion were invalid, so money was often left to a trustee who had separate instructions for its use. It was also illegal for clergy ordained overseas to minister to members of their religion, so it was necessary to resort to Anglican clergy for civil functions. Was the steward of Tern, who was buried at Atcham that November, in fact a Catholic? There is a further link between the Hills and the Smythes: Maria's second husband, Henry Errington, brother of Sir Edward's sister-in-law, was from a Catholic family in Northumberland. Some years earlier Sir Edward's brother Walter had been living at Tong where his eldest child, Maria Anne, who was now seventeen, was born. The family now lived in Hampshire, near Errington's estate of Redrice. Maria Anne was later Mrs Fitzherbert, morganatic wife of George IV.

Bell was succeeded as house steward by Richard Partridge, who had worked for Godolphin Edwards of Frodesley Park until Edwards' death in 1772. He kept a book of Memoranda where he recorded that he had been to Tern on 8 October 1773 to speak to Noel Hill and Mr Hurd. John Hurd, of Hatton Grange, looked after the whole estate. Partridge's service began on 12 October; his family joined him at Tern before Bell's death. Hurd reported to Thomas Hill early in 1774: 'The bills at Tern run pretty high, upon your son's perusal of them, I find he is come to a resolution to lessen the number of his horses, hounds and servts which I am very glad of and hope he will be no otherwise expensive in his household affairs than is consistent with the dignity of your son. Any further alterations in buildings etc: I believe will not be wanted, and no more labourers kept than are absolutely necessary, all which I thought proper to make you acquainted with not doubting but it will be a great satisfaction.' The letter is endorsed in Thomas Hill's hand: 'that Mr Child had disbanded his huntsmen and dogs and horses I hoped he wd endeavr to perswade N. Hill to follow his example.' As it happens, we have a letter of N. Hill's, to the younger John Oliver, who was not only his financial manager, but also his friend. It is dated 18 February, and deals with money and estate matters: 'I am much obliged to you for your friendship in talking to Dr Adams about the exchanges which ought to take place between my Neighbours Calcotts and myself; I mentioned it to Mr Hurd in my way to Town he made more difficulty than I expected but however I think no time should be lost while my Neighbours are ready and willing to oblige me; you was perfectly right in saying that I could not do without the Pinfold piece as unless exchanges are made at first in a liberal and handsome manner they seldom afterwards take place.' After more business, he ends on a familiar note: 'My friend Leighton has again experienced that London Gallantry is dangerous; my Father never looked better and is I think in perfect good humour and I find matters wear a smooth Face to me in every Respect. I hope the Hounds go on well.' If Oliver should go to Tern, he said, he would be glad to know how things were. Vernon was also with them at Cleveland Court: 'he has married Charlotte to some good Body but he does not own it is to his Footman.' Unfortunately, we know nothing of Charlotte. We have an indication of the size of Hill's household at Tern, from a list in Hurd's hand: fourteen manservants, from the steward at an annual wage of £40 to the house boy at £5; huntsman, groom, whipper-in, stable boys and dog feeder; women servants from the housekeeper at £20 a year to the still maid and dairy maid at £5 each. A 'Gouvernante', at £20 a year, four nursemaids, and 21 labourers complete the list. Wages and board wages totalled £979 a year.

Noel Hill did not seem to be planning economies at this time, but some servants did leave his service that year. One was James, the children's friend; another was William Bennett. His accounts were examined and signed by himself and Noel Hill for the last time on 31 December 1774. But the admirable butler did not go far. He succeeded Vincent Quantin as inn-keeper of the Talbot, near Tern Hall. A notice appeared the following May, in the *Shrewsbury Chronicle*: 'William Bennett, late Butler to Noel Hill Esq: begs leave to inform the Public that he has taken, and entered upon, that commodious Inn, known by the sign of the Talbot in Atcham, where he humbly solicits their patronage.' His name appears in the Register of Recognizances of Alehouse Licencees from 1775 to 1778. Noel Hill had the inn and house rebuilt for him by Lee and Scoltock, and new dining tables made, including a large table in the bargemen's room. The mason, Charles Lloyd, made a chimney piece of Grinshill stone. The workmen included Edward and John Harding, John Nichols, Phil Jones, Sam Becket and Thomas Shakeshaft. Stucco work was done by Josiah Bromfield; Mr Davies, the upholdster, did the house out in fine sky-blue, yellow, and green and white paper. Was this house also architect-designed? Mylne's diary has the entry for 10 March 1774: 'Gave Mr Hill an alteration of a Cottage and drawing of gate adjoining with advice about river, mill, etc.' Another visit was made to Tern in June that year, as Mylne records: 'at Tern. Rode round the Ground, recomend altering the aproach and Roads to House taking away Mill, making Entrance on East side of House, altering stairs etc.'

Certain exchanges of land and alterations to roads and paths were effected as part of Hill's plans for his estate. The Shropshire Quarter Sessions in April 1773 recorded that Noel Hill had been granted a licence 'to inclose a certain Highway leading from Tern Bridge to Berwick Maviston to Upton Magna . . . And also to stop up a certain Footpath leading from Tern Bridge over a certain piece of Ground of the said Noel Hill in Tern . . and from thence over certain other pieces of land of the said Noel Hill in Berwick Maviston . . . And also to stop up a certain footpath leading from the Blacksmith's Shop in Atcham through a garden of the said Noel Hill in the possession of Ann

Farnolds Widow [of the blacksmith] and over certain other lands of Noel Hill . . .' This part of the road, going northwards to Berwick Maviston, was 1276 yards long and six yards broad; another part of the road, from Berwick to Upton Magna, 'ending at the North Corner of a Plantation of the said Noel Hill in Tern' was about 880 yards long and eight yards broad. Hill was to make alternative highways in the parish of Atcham, and there were no objections. His brother-in-law Robert Burton had lately given him a piece of land. Hill had not yet finished his improvements to Tern, nor did he adopt the measures advocated by his eighty year old father. Noel Hill's status as a country gentleman was about to be enhanced, and there would be no reduction of the Style which his Situation, as he had described it, required.

Chapter 5
Knight of the Shire

Politics was in the Shropshire air again in 1773. A general election was due by March 1775, when the seven year term of the parliament would be up. In 1772 one of the county members, Sir John Astley, had died, and been replaced by young Sir Watkin Williams Wynn; there had been criticism of an 'outsider' representing Shropshire, but Sir Watkin would be standing for Denbighshire next time. Lord Clive had wanted a county seat; in 1772 he had succeeded Lord Powis as Lord Lieutenant, but did not have his power. Some wondered if Sir Harry Bridgeman would try again. Another with his eye on the vacancy was John Mytton who offered himself for the county at any time. During 1773 Clive was under attack in Parliament from those who felt his activities in Bengal should be investigated. Debates were fierce in May and Clive made some notable speeches in his own defence. Horace Walpole recorded, in his *Last Journals*, that Clive ended his speech on the 21st with the appeal that 'they would leave him his honour, and take away his fortune'. Debate continued after Clive left to wait at home for the result of the motion that he had abused his powers. 'At four in the morning the House divided, and the motion was rejected by 153 to 95. To complete Clive's triumph . . . the House voted next, at the instigation of the Solicitor-General, that Robert Lord Clive had rendered great and meritorious service to this country.' Noel Hill was by this time in the country but he had a letter from Ashby; the Corporation of Shrewsbury met on 25 May to draw up a congratulatory address to Clive. The following spring, Hill was in the country from mid-March to mid-April, when moves were afoot to select him as member for the county, with Charles Baldwyn. A 'knight of the shire' had more prestige than a borough member, being selected by his fellow gentlemen.

He kept a letter book for the period 10 March to 21 May, so we can see something of the process. One of the first letters was from old Brooke Forester, who wrote from Stone in Staffordshire, on his way to Buxton. From Buxton he wrote again to say he had sent letters to Sir Harry Bridgeman, Colonel Davenant, Lord Kilmorey, Mr Smitheman, Mr Charlton, Mr Corbet of the Park (Shawbury Park) and to his son. The Foresters controlled both of the Much Wenlock seats, though Brooke had now resigned his. His son George also gave his support to Hill, writing from Willey Park on 10 April: 'The bearer brings the hound you desired and you are welcome to keep him as long as life remains to enable him to do the stallion business . . . he has been an uncommon good hound . . . his name is dancer.' As for the political matter, he promised to 'summon the small but faithful circle of friends in this neighbourhood, and I'll be bound for it they serve you without one dissenting voice.' He was one of the heartiest of squires. The *English Chronicle*, quoted in *The History of Parliament*, claimed that George Forester owed his repeated election to the good opinions he won through his liberality and his ability as a magistrate. 'He is eminently distinguished for the two prescriptive characteristics of an English gentleman, an attachment to the chase, and a generous hospitality at the conclusion of it.' George Forester's Fieldingesque qualities extended to his dealings with women; he never married, but fathered many children, for whom, with their mothers, he provided. In his letter to Noel Hill he referred to his relations with his father. 'I have ever been excluded from that confidential capacity I shou'd have wished to have enjoy'd with my Father both in private as well as on publick affairs.' As it happens, we know the circumstances of the rift between the two from a letter of Thomas Bell's, written in December 1759. 'Verry Probably you may have heard of the Extraordinary affair that has happened in the Dottell [Dothill] family. Mr George Forrester has got Patty Riding off his Father and has her at Willey and will not part with her, he has been frequently with her at Dottell in his Father's absence for several weeks past of which the Father was made acquainted by the Chamber Maid about Wednesday last, the day following he catched a Messenger with a Bundle in which was her Gold Watch Ear rings etc and a Letter appointing time and place where George was to meet her and carry her off. Upon this his father sent a servant with her to Shrewsbury and from there she got to Willy next morning, they say this has made such a Breach between Father and son as is not likely to be made up. A good many People have made themselves Verry Merry upon this occation.'

Another supporter of Noel Hill was Edward Rogers of Eaton Mascott, a former Sheriff of Shropshire (in 1764). He hoped that 'our neighbours at Cund' (Cound) might be attached: 'tho your neighbours have no great interest yet I think a candidate cuts a better figure so supported tho' it should not be with numbers.' He advised that, as the matter was now 'pretty publick', Hill should himself apply to people. He had been to Tern while Noel was there, but they had been busy with these affairs. In Hill's absence he had taken 'a peep at your improvements . . . the ground not being finish'd nor in verdure, and trees very low, looks like a fair land to my dim eyes; I suppose you have a plan of it that one may see.' Hill now informed Clive, who was in Geneva, after a tour to Italy, that he had received great encouragement to offer himself for the county. Clive replied, thanking Hill and hoping that he would keep matters quiet in Shrewsbury for him. The old enemy Pulteney also wrote to Hill to say that he understood that 'the gentlemen of Shropshire, your friends and neighbours, have resolved unsolicited and uninfluenced, to propose you for the County, a very flattering mark of their respect and one of the highest which an independent in this County can aspire to.' He hoped for Hill's support in the Shrewsbury election. Noel later described this letter as 'Jesuitical and Bargaining', written at a time when Pulteney was canvassing against him. Hill also wrote to Sir Rowland Hill, hoping for his support if none of the Hawkstone family was thinking of standing. Sir Rowland replied that he had given his word not to engage himself before the county meeting, but was under no engagement which could be prejudicial to Noel's interest. Support came from others: Sir Richard Acton invited him to Aldenham at any time; Ned Kynaston's widow promised a sincere welcome at Hardwick 'if you can drink humble port, and eat mutton and chickens.' Mr Flint (later Corbett) wrote that he was happy that things 'flow so agreeable in the Country . . . even your friend Mr Mytton's subterfuges should rather impel than impede.' Mytton was openly hostile, but he had after all once offered his own services; an announcement in the *Shrewsbury Chronicle* of July that year stated that he declined the honour of offering himself — but the choice of the gentlemen had been made by then so he had no other option.

Noel and his family were back in the country in time for the Whitchurch Races on 25 and 26 May. These occasions, when gentlemen could discuss county matters, had an added importance in an election year. In June they visited Hardwick, at Mrs Kynaston's invitation. Later in the month they were occupied for three days at the Bridgnorth Races, where one of the stewards that year was Charlton Leighton. Early in July Mrs Hill visited her family at Hilton; she was expecting a fifth child in the autumn. The Shrewsbury Assizes came on in July, the Caractacus meeting on 1 August, and the Shrewsbury Races from 23 to 26 of that month. It was during this meeting that the *Shrewsbury Chronicle* announced that Noel Hill had 'this Day been unanimously approved as a proper Person to represent the County in the ensuing Parliament.' The Gentlemen, Freeholders and Clergy of the county had been summoned to meet in the Town Hall, by the Sheriff, Robert Pigott, to nominate their representatives. So, at the age of twenty-nine, Noel Hill was accorded a signal honour. He and Charles Baldwyn advertised their thanks, and Charlton Leighton, from Loton, announced his application to the burgesses to replace Noel Hill as member for the borough. Clive and Pulteney would also be standing.

The *Shrewsbury Chronicle* announced social as well as electoral affairs. The stewards of the races had advertised: no one was to be admitted to the assemblies without a ticket, which could be obtained at the Coffee House, the Talbot or the Raven; ladies' tickets for three nights cost five shillings, gentlemens' seven shillings and sixpence. The ordinaries, or dinners, for the men and ladies were separate, taking place in rotation at the Talbot and the Raven. With the autumn season approaching, the players returned to the Theatre in Shrewsbury. Mr Miller had been bringing his actors since 1772, but his name is less prominent in the 1774 announcements. 'On Monday, August 22, will be presented the celebrated Dramatic Romance call'd CYMON . . . Sylvia by Mrs Raworth (from the Theatre-Royal, York) . . . on Tuesday a Tragedy call'd the ROYAL CONVERT . . .' Politics were not entirely excluded: 'By Desire of Mrs Pulteney . . . On Monday, August 29, will be performed a concert of vocal and instrumental MUSIC . . . the celebrated Masque call'd COMUS . . . To which will be added a Farce call'd the MOCK DOCTOR.' Something to suit all tastes; the Pulteneys were enormously wealthy and could well afford such sponsorship. The season continued with *Hamlet, King Henry IV, The Provoked Husband*, the tragedies *Alonzo, Isabella, or the Fatal Marriage, Henry II, or the Fall of Rosamond* (a new scene of Rosamond's bower was included); then a *tour de force* by Mrs Hunter who acted Lady Macbeth and the Irish Widow on the same bill.

In late September, Noel Hill and his wife returned to London. On the 30th the Cabinet announced an immediate election — it was to be held on 11 October in Shrewsbury so Noel had to return to help his friend Leighton, and to vote. Anne Hill was quite practised at having children now, this being her fifth, but she probably had her mother and one or more of her sisters with her

The Shrewsbury Election, 1774 — the Town Hall Square. *(Local Studies Library, Shrewsbury)*

as she went to Hilton afterwards. Her sister-in-law, Maria, was not in Town, but was travelling abroad. The Earl of Derby wrote to Lady Gower that he had been at Lady Broughton's, in Lausanne: 'she and Mr Errington are here a few weeks on their way to Italy to consult Dr Tissot on account of her health.' (They all considered the Swiss extremely ungainly dancers, compared to the French.) He had been 'a great deal with Lady Broughton, whom I like vastly.' Anne Hill's child was born on 11 October, another son, who was named Richard. On the same day a lively election began in Shrewsbury. After the reading of the Sheriff's Precept to the mayor, Thomas Loxdale, John Ashby, the town clerk, administered the oath to the returning officer; it was agreed that voters should be brought up in fives. The lawyers now had their day, representing the various parties and arguing the eligibility of the voters. The first of these was one William Humphreys: Mr Davenport, for Leighton, argued that he was not an inhabitant; Mr Kenyon, for Pulteney, argued the niceties of the definition; Mr Jones, for the mayor, answered Kenyon. Humphreys, it appeared, was a resident in Montgomeryshire and had been in Shrewsbury only a week; his vote was rejected. On 12 October, Noel Hill was objected to by Mr Kenyon: he replied that although he lived at Tern he had had lodgings in town since the last election, at Mr Lacon Bennett's, near the Market House; further, he was assessed for a stable at his father's, which could hold six horses, and which he used when he was in town. He was admitted to vote. After three days the results were announced: Clive, 221 votes; Leighton, 179; Pulteney, 171. Pulteney resorted to the *Chronicle*: 'I thank you for the great Number of Votes which you have given me, and altho' the Returning Officer has thought proper to reject a Number of Burgesses which I think are legal Voters . . . [I am] resolved to present a Petition to the

House of Commons as soon as the Parliament meets.' A 'Correspondent' observed, in the same newspaper: 'It is remarkable that during the late Poll for the Town, the Inhabitants in general took frequent Opportunities of expressing their wishes in favour of Mr Pulteney . . . when he had declared his Resolution to petition the House of Commons, they in great Crowds carried him along the Streets, to the Raven-Inn, in a Chair, elegantly ornamented with the choicest Flowers, with Colours flying, and every Demonstration of an almost frantic Joy . . .' Each candidate had his own colours, for partisans to sport.

At the end of the month Mrs Hill returned home, after a short stay at Hilton, where Noel met her. He wrote to his father from Tern on 4 November: 'Mrs Hill got down to Hilton very well as also the young Child and they both continue so; our time passed very pleasently there as many friends met us. On our return home, we were much chagrined to find little Anne not well and has continued so for some Days, Mrs Hill desires you will excuse on this account her not having wrote to you as she has been with the Child continually who now is much recovered, all the others are perfectly well.' He added that they were delaying their return to London until after Christmas: 'my Wife does not recover her strength so fast as usual and wishes to stay

Sir Charlton Leighton, fourth Baronet, (d. 1784), MP for Shrewsbury 1780–84.
(Loton Park. Photograph Paul Stamper)

quietly in the country a little while.' If Parliamentary business should call, he would, of course, not neglect his duty. Parliament met on 29 November, but Shrewsbury had not finished with its election affairs. With Pulteney petitioning, Noel Hill stood by his friend Leighton. He defended his actions to his father, who must have voiced some criticism. In a letter of 24 November Noel made a firm statement: 'The resentment which Mr P—— and his agents think proper to show is unmerited, I have done nothing more than endeavoured to serve a friend with whom I have been bred up from my Infancy and to whose connections as well as to himself I was under obligations for their voluntary offers of assistance in the County . . . I found Mr Leighton encouraged to offer his Services by many respectable Gentlemen in the Town and in the Neighbourhood. I thought I acted uniformly in conjunction with my friends when I joined the services I could render him to theirs; some indeed fell far short of their promises but [I] had rather the whole of the Resentment shown to me than to have been less active than I have been once I had promised to assist a friend.' On 4 December, in a letter dealing with estate business, Noel mentions that 'Mr P—— has wrote a letter excusing himself from coming to Salop immediately on account of Mrs P—— Health; in the meantime the Candidates continue their Canvass with spirits.'

Pulteney arrived on 17 December, from London; the *Chronicle* reported that 'He was met at Atcham by upwards of a Hundred Gentlemen and Tradesmen, who accompanied him in procession to the Raven-Inn: They were preceded into Town by a Band of Music, with Flags.' Pulteney had won his Mandamus case against the Corporation — and been hailed by an unknown bard in a Song in Commemoration of 19th November:

> Auspicious day brave boys Rejoyce
> Upon this Just Occasion
> The Corporation on our Rights
> Had made a vile Invasion
> Till Pulteney Brave did set us free
> This day we will remember
> To keep it let us all agree
> The Nineteenth of November.

Something of the spirit of faction that George III complained of in his American colonies had got into the citizens of Shrewsbury. There was another event to complicate the issue, and excite speculation: on 22 November, in London, Clive, in a fit of agonizing pain, had killed himself. His parliamentary seat was thus vacant before the session began.

On 30 December Noel Hill wrote: 'The same Plan of preserving the Peace of the Town as occurred to you [Thomas Hill] and others in London had been adopted by the Gentlemen here. I send you a copy of an Invitation signed by Messrs Tayleurs Kynaston Dr Hart Rocke etc unanimously agreed on at a meeting held at the Town Hall on Monday and sent of by express. Mr Mytton attended the meeting and treated the Peace of the Town as a ridiculous cant expression lately adopted in this Country, and supports his Nephew Corbett. I did not attend the meeting as I wished to take no active part in this matter, the Gentlemen and my Friends however sent for me and desired me to attend . . . The Resentment shewn by Mr M—— and his Nephew to Mr L—— and myself and the Inclination shewn to inflame have done them great prejudice with the Gentlemen.' In the following March a court ruling was made in favour of Pulteney, who was seated in place of Leighton. He came once more to Shrewsbury in triumph, and supported Corbet who was elected in Clive's place. As the *Victoria County History* notes: 'Pulteney had carried both seats and had put an end to the corporation's control of the franchise and to the Clive interest. He was to sit for Shrewsbury for thirty years, unopposed at five general elections.' When Corbet retired in 1780, Leighton succeeded him.

Meanwhile, in the autumn of 1774, the round of entertainment went on. A varied repertoire was shown at the Theatre — Noel Hill's servants were treated to Miller's benefit (*Macbeth* plus *The Irish Widow*), and Carleton's (the new comedy, *The School for Wives*). The Hills themselves were back at Tern in time to see the last performances of the season: *The Beggar's Opera, Richard III, Cato*, and, finally, for the benefit of Master Remington and Master and Miss Phillips, the tragedy *Theodosius, or The Force of Love*. A notice in the newspaper reveals that backstage rivalry had occupied the players, while the townspeople were fighting elections. Mr and Mrs Phillips were taking over the Company after Mr Miller said he would not be again concerned with the management, but they protested that they had not opposed Mr Miller. Mrs Phillips, conscious of the favours of the ladies and gentlemen of Shrewsbury, assured them 'while they think her worthy to Appear before them, no Theatrical Station of Life she may be placed in, shall ever prevent her from Annually paying her Respects here.'

Conflict on a larger stage came to the fore during 1775, as the situation with regard to America worsened. Horace Walpole's *Last Journals* reflect the feelings in Parliament. In March 1774 one member of the Commons had declared the 'claims and pretentions of the Americans had gone beyond all example, and that the question now was whether the colonies were any longer to belong to Britain; that the best blood of this country had been sacrificed in their defence, and yet that the expected advantages were not to be maintained without asserting our sovereignty.' North was anxious to 'secure a proper dependence of the colonies'; Burke warned that 'A combination of all the colonies would ensue'.

In July 1775 the American answer came with the battle of Bunker Hill; the war had begun, but as yet the life of country gentry was not affected. The militia were more concerned with balls than with battles. Noel Hill had had a new uniform made in London — scarlet coat with green lapels, cuffs and collars, a white waistcoat and breeches, gold epaulettes and gilt buttons — for the militia ball at the Raven in the autumn. Before that came the races: Mrs Hill went with her husband to Bridgnorth in June; her brother Henry's horse, Doubtful, came second in his race. At Shrewsbury in August their uncle Richard's Little Putnam came second, but brother-in-law Grosvenor had two winners. One of Henry Vernon's horses was named Matchless Penelope — perhaps a compliment to the lady he married in October that year. (Horses were a serious passion with Vernon, as with his uncle Richard with whom he often stayed at Newmarket — 'this *agreable place*' he called it in a letter to Nicholas Smyth in October 1774. This letter is entirely concerned with horses: an expensive purchase of his uncle's, and one of his own, had gone lame. 'In this life we are born to meet with misfortunes', he reflected; 'you have few, you are well mounted in all respects and I hope Ratoni will be one of the many comforts you may enjoy.' Vernon had sold Ratoni to Smyth — he hoped Smyth would not part with him.

Vernon's wife, Penelope Graham, was the daughter of a Dublin gentleman. In November 1775 the Hills met her for the first time at Hilton. Mrs Hill wrote to Thomas Hill on 20 November: 'My Brother seems very happy and I like my sister-in-law very much. from the little judgement I was able to form in one day . . she appears to be very good-humour'd and is sensible and well-bred, they come here next week.' After the return visit, Noel endorsed his wife's opinion. He wrote on 4 December: 'Mr and Mrs Vernon came here last week the Family from Acton Burnell Mr and Mrs Congreve General Severne Mrs Smith of Condover have been here to wait on them. Mrs Vernon appears to be a well-bred sensible good Tempered woman. The weather has been remarkably mild and fine since we have been here . . . every one in Salop are unanimous against the Americans and approve much the Conduct of those who supported Government in Parliament.' Mrs Smith of Condover was the former Miss Leighton, Charlton's sister Anna Maria, who had married his and Noel's friend Nicholas Smyth (a former Captain in the Gloucestershire Militia). The visiting continued. Noel wrote to his father on 28 December: 'I never was in better Health and have been so ever since I have been in the Country. Mrs Hill and I have been for ten days at Loton on a visit to Mr and Mrs Child they are now with us.' His friend Charlton was now living at Loton and the Childes were his sister Annabella and her husband William.

Back in London, the Hills' last child was born on 28 March 1776. In September she was baptized at Atcham, Amelia Louisa; she was known as Emily. That winter Penelope Vernon was expecting a child. Noel and Anne called at Hilton after an overnight visit to Weston Park (where a 'Magnificent Entertainment' was put on) and were detained there, 'Mrs Vernon being unfortunately brought to Bed . . of a Dead Child; my Wife's care was thought necessary and Vernon's spirits being very low I could not well leave him.' Having volunteered to act as Foreman on the Jury of the Borough Quarter Sessions, he had to be back in Shrewsbury on 17 January. He wrote to his father: 'I beleive Mr Mayor was well pleased . . Compliments were paid the Jury from the Bench. 27 served on the Jury and we dined together, more than Double the number ever known on such an occasion.' The Quarter Sessions records show that Robert Corbett, the Mayor, John Langley, Thomas Fownes and Robert More, a former mayor, were on the Bench. Of the long list of those summoned to serve on the grand Jury, the 'jurats', who actually served, numbered twenty-seven, as Hill said. He heads the list, as Foreman, and among the others were Samuel Sandford, surgeon, Francis Lloyd (of Leaton), Edmund Littlehales, Plowden Slaney, Joshua Eddowes (printer and stationer), John Oliver the younger, and various farmers and tradesmen — merchants, mercers, a butcher and a brazier, a hatter, an upholdster and an apothecary. The business was not arduous, most constables reporting that they had nothing to present and that all was 'fair and well'. Mary Pinches pleaded not guilty to stealing a silver teaspoon from Mrs Adams, but was ordered to be privately whipped. William Birch of Bicton, accused of assaulting John Mansell, was fined sixpence, which he paid in court. Four other people were discharged.

Another example of Hill's service as a public figure was a Bill in Parliament — a matter of 'private Busyness' referred to in his letter to his father; he would return to London and parliamentary duties the following week, he said. The business had been discussed in Shrewsbury at the Guildhall on 15 January, having been announced in the *Shrewsbury Chronicle:* 'whereas the present Laws are thought to be ineffectual for the Preservation of the Fish in the River Severn, several Gentlemen [are] desirous that a Public Meeting may be called.' Robert Pemberton, a prominent attorney in the town, collected opinions which he forwarded to Hill in February. John Owens, a Montgomeryshire farmer, recalled that salmon used to be plentiful, but had for some years been scarce. The fish went up-river to spawn from August to November, but were being taken by night poachers, with lights and spears; 'it is frequently the diversion of Servants and Idle people.' John Bradley of Bridgnorth testified that for the past twelve or fourteen years, the salmon catchers down-river, below Gloucester Bridge, had been fixing longer nets than before, with smaller meshes, and dragging the river so that the salmon could scarcely escape. They were also destroying the supply of lampreys and elvers. It was agreed that a new Bill was needed, to cover the Vyrnwy as well as the Severn: killing by spears must be stopped; the fords should not be dragged; elvers, lampreys and salmon fry must be protected. Offenders should be liable to summary penalties, and informers should be given power to act as witnesses. Angling, however, 'which is more a Matter of Amusement', was not objected to. On 19 April a meeting was held in London, at the Star and Garter, Pall Mall, where it was agreed that a Bill should be applied for early in the next session of Parliament for Regulating and Improving the Fishery in the Severn; that all the Members of Parliament concerned should be notified, as well as the Clerks of the Peace, and that the decision should be published in the Birmingham, Shrewsbury, Gloucester, Worcester and Hereford papers. A contrary bill by Gloucester was opposed. When the Fishery Bill was put on the Statute Book in 1778 these demands were incorporated.

Summer once more brought the country race meetings; of particular importance to Hill in 1777 was the meeting at Oswestry early in July. It was held at Cyrn y Bwch, with dinners for the ladies and gentlemen each day, balls at night, and a public breakfasting on the Bowling Green on the second race day. Sir Henry Bridgeman and Charles Baldwyn acted as stewards. The 'intelligence from Oswestry', published in the *Shrewsbury Chronicle* the following day, was eloquent. 'On the 3d and 4th instant was held the second meeting since the revival of our races . . . where the number, lustre, and unanimity of the company, promise the most flouring success to the re-establishment of this diversion here, in which there is something peculiarly agreeable arising from an unparalleled circumstance of picturesque beauty: for between the intervals of sports, you are entertained with one of the most extensive and lively scenes of landscape that can be imagined . . . The cup, given by Sir Watkin Williams Wynn, Bart, which is very magnificent, was won by a hunter belonging to Noel Hill Esq, and afterwards by him presented to our Mayor and Corporation, in return for which act of generosity, he was unanimously elected a Burgess of this Town and Borough.' Hill and Watkin Williams Esq were appointed stewards for the following year, 'and as they have done us the honour to accept the nomination, we doubt not they will be genteelly attended.' The silver cup is indeed magnificent, and still the prized

The Oswestry Race Cup, 1777,
won by Noel's horse, Little Malton,
presented by him to
Oswestry Town Council. *(Oswestry Town Council)*

possession of Oswestry. It has an additional inscription: 'The Gift of Noel Hill Esq. to the Corporation of Oswestry, Won by his Horse Young Malton.' This bay hunter beat two other horses to win the fifty guineas cup. Two years later Noel Hill was chosen mayor of Oswestry, having been mayor of Shrewsbury the preceding year.

In August 1777 there was a visit to Scarborough, possibly on account of Mrs Hill's health, as we learn from the butler's petty cash book that she went sea-bathing. A bathing dress 'for Mistress' cost 17/6d; bathing was one guinea, with 10/6d for the Bathing woman. Lodgings for three weeks came to £18.18s.0d, and the servants were paid board wages. On the return journey to Shropshire they may have visited Wentworth Woodhouse in South Yorkshire, as there is an entry at the end of the month for payment of a guinea to Lord Rockingham's groom, perhaps for bringing a horse from the Marquis's famous stables. (Young Malton's name suggests that he too may have been a Rockingham colt.) From this time on we find occasional evidence of Anne Hill's ill-health: a journey to Bath in January 1780, bathing on the Isle of Wight the following summer, and Clifton Wells two years later. References to the children usually report that they are well, with only minor ailments. They were now old enough for their education to be undertaken.

On 8 August 1775 John Fletcher of Madeley had written to Charles Wesley. 'I am going to see Mr Hill my quondam pupil who is now member for this county, and who wants me to educate his son. I thought he had had enough of me. I go to put off the unwelcome charge.' Thomas Noel — Tommy — was nearly five at the time, a little younger than Noel when Fletcher first went to Cleveland Court as tutor. Whether through Fletcher or not, a foreign tutor was found for the children, a Mr De Linat, who is mentioned in a letter dated 10 December 1777, from Noel to his father. 'We got here [Tern] yesterday by one o'clock with great ease and had a good Jorney; we had the satisfaction of finding the Children all perfectly well, Harriot is quite recovered, she and Ann and William enquired much after you and particularly after their brother Tom . . . Mr De Linat has been Ill and is extremely pulled down by it. he attributes his illness to catching Cold by laying in a damp bed at the Raven in Shrewsbury a few days before we left Tern.' The journey south may have been made to take Tom to school, at Epsom — he had had his seventh birthday in October. At first one of the servants, Elizabeth Gittins, stayed there to look after him; she was paid board wages from June to November that year, as well as an allowance for the boy. 'Master Hills bills' cover such items as material, thread and buttons for shirts (doubtless made by Mrs Gittins), gloves, a hat, buckles, hair cuts, soap, paper, wax, pens and ink, letters and brimstone treacle. A tailor made his green "cassimere" suits, with silk trimmings, and a sateen great frock (frock coat) with a velvet collar. Eight pairs of shoes were made for him by Andrew Johnston, shoemaker, of Cranbourne Street. The bill, for £1.14s.9d, included two pairs of toed clogs for Miss Hill (Henrietta) who was put into stays, with Anne (now five); they had muslin frocks made, and their slippers were of black leather, red morocco, and green leather bound with red. Master and Miss Hill also had pumps made, probably for their dancing lessons. Later on, William joined his brother at school.

It may have been at that time that Mr De Linat's employment with Noel Hill finished. He seems to have had a romantic and Rousseauesque feeling for the children, to judge from a letter he wrote to Thomas Hill (though we must allow for some flattery as he may have hoped to get another situation through Hill). 'I write in *French* to the lovely Miss Henrietta, and to the Lively Miss Nancy; nothing can interest me more than their progress in all accomplishments. Nature has been very kind and lavish of its favours to these two promising young Ladies, and to all the charming young Family. can I take the liberty to request that, when you'll be at Tern, you will please, Sir, remember me to them. I am more sincerely attached to every one of them, and cannot express how désagréeable and irksome the separation seems to me! I had contracted the pleasing habit of seeing them daily, and living in the family with them — to suspend or break off a dear habit is not the work of a day. the company of such a fine and amiable little génération is more entertaining for any rational being who will examine the éxertions of Nature and the progress of education, than is commonly imagined — the Two young gentlemen, Messrs Thomas and William, are very well, appear to be greatly pleased with their situation. I saw their Master, recommended and entreated him to use them well, assured him that nothing would contribute more to his own satisfaction, and to their improvement, than the best, most civil and mildest treatment.' It is to be hoped that the master at Epsom did not resent this Gallic advice on education. The lively Miss Nancy, young Anne, was able to compose a very fluent letter in French to her 'Cher gran Papa' when she was about seven, staying with her parents and brother William at Hastings, in July 1778. 'Votre petite Nanette' was in high spirits, happier than a queen. She asked her grandfather to give messages to 'la Chere Emilie, et au gros Richard' at Tern — these, the babies of the family, were now aged two and three respectively. A draft reply from Thomas Hill to the tutor, dated 17 September 1778 and addressed to Bath, wishes him success and acknowledges his merits. He gives news of the family, saying that the children are all well 'and greatly obliged to you and I hope will always remember with Respectful Gratitude your tender indulgence to them.' A memorandum records Hill's intention to remind Noel to 'write to Mr Fletcher to send over a proper person for a Tutor', so that clergyman may well have recommended de Linat.

Of the children's studies we have few details, but can assume that, as well as French and proficiency in reading and writing their own language, the girls were taught the usual accomplishments — needlework, drawing and painting, dancing and music. Henrietta was taught music by the celebrated Dr Burney, as we shall see. The scholarly doctor's three volume study of *The State of Music in France, Italy etc* was in the Hills' library. Other books published in the 1770s and also in their possession included *fables* and *contes* of La Fontaine, Bryant's *Ancient Mythology*, Fénelon's *Aventures de Télémaque*, Goldsmith's *History of England*, Moore's *Fables for the Female Sex*, and the letters of Lady Rachel Russell and Madame de Sévigné. Devis's *Lessons for Young Ladies* and Lady Pennington's *Advice to her Daughters* were added later. As well as books of 'educational' value, there were many others, on subjects ranging from law and politics to poetry and gardens. Chaucer, Spenser, Shakespeare and his contemporaries, Collins and Gray were all there. Hill's particular interests are represented: Adair's *History of the American Indians*, Burke's *European Settlements in America*, Carver's *Travels in North America*, Bolt's *Considerations on Indian Affairs*, Douglas's *History of Controverted Elections*, Hatsell's *Precedents of Proceedings in Parliament*, in four volumes. There were Arthur Young's *Farmers' Letters* and *A Tour through the Southern Counties of England;* Kent's *Hints to Gentlemen of Landed Property;* Heeley's *Beauties of Hagley, Enville and Leasowes.* There were also two copies of Phillips' *History of Shrewsbury*, published in 1779, and dedicated to Noel Hill, mayor the previous year.

During 1778 the Hills moved from Cleveland Court to a more fashionable part of London, leasing a house in Sackville Street. A reference to its having been lately in the possession of Lord Stamford identifies the house as No. 30, on the pleasanter west side of the street. *The Survey of London* gives a description: 'a large house of the 1730s . . . with a front of three storeys, five windows wide'. Sackville Street, the Survey tells us, 'must have been very attractive when first built, its width of about 42 feet being generously proportioned to the houses, mostly of three storeys, with fairly uniform fronts of simple design, built of good stock brick with stone dressings'. The west side adjoined the spacious gardens of Sunderland House, with the larger grounds of Burlington House beyond. Although not in the first rank of fashion, the larger houses, particularly on the west side, 'attracted throughout the eighteenth century the minor nobility, the dowager, the member of Parliament, the senior army officer and the prosperous medical man.' One of the last was Dr Warren, physician to the Prince of Wales. Even then, though, there were some shops: two apothecaries and a cheesemonger, and one tavern and a coffee house. While the Hills moved in, the two older girls, Harriet and Anne, were taken care of by the servants out of town, at Earls Court: Elizabeth Gittins was paid twelve weeks board wages. The youngest children were apparently with their parents — the milk bill includes 'nursery milk'. Housekeeping accounts for this time show regular payments to butcher, cheesemonger, grocer, fishmonger, chandler, poulterer, baker, greengrocer and oilman. A month's bills, from 28 January to 23 February 1777, amounted to £71.2s.9¾d. The oilman was situated conveniently near when they moved to Sackville Street; William Mackay, Oil-Man at the Olive Tree, opposite Burlington House, Piccadilly. He provided a wide range of goods, apart from various oils: vinegar, mustard, salt, macaroni, vermicelli, anchovies, truffles, morellos, 'parmezan', hams, isinglas, fullers earth, ivory black, powder blue, starch, packing thread, and paper and brooms. The grocer purveyed green tea, Turkish coffee, chocolate, Lisbon sugar, rice, currants, raisins, nutmegs, black pepper. Meat and greengroceries were varied. Separately accounted were the wine bills, on quite a lavish scale. Not surprisingly, apothecaries' bills were regular — normal disorders were aggravated by rich living; gout was one of Noel's troubles, as well as the bilious complaint of long standing. Newspapers were delivered — the London ones and the Courier de l'Europe.

Bills for clothes from 1777 and 1778 show what the fashionable were wearing. A. Mathias, mantua-maker, was paid £6.4s.9¼d for making a marone corded tabby (a rich, watered silk) Italian gown and coat, a corded tabby French jacket and coat, altering a tabby dress and flowered silk sack, and making a white masquerade dress. A French mantua-maker, M Flamand, made Mrs Hill silk dresses of 'la Persienne' and Italian style, a 'habit de Cour', and white déshabille and petticoat. Lace was bought from M Bruquier; Elizabeth Guerint provided gauze handkerchiefs and caps, one dress cap having gold spangles. Mary Massal was paid six guineas for a black hat and a cap with feathers. John Nicholls, shoemaker, made silk slippers of various colours, decorated with roses. Noel's tailor, William Fell, of St Martin's Lane, made a fawn frock coat and breeches, silver and tabby waistcoat (with a Welsh flannel under waistcoat), a striped silk and quilted waistcoat, a silver tissue waistcoat, a fawn velvet coat and straw silk waistcoat, a Bath coating greatcoat with velvet collar and facings, a blue cloth frock coat with scarlet Genoa collar (probably for hunting), and a brown holland powdering gown. To ride in, in their fine clothes, they had a new landau, made by Mr Wright, coachmaker. The bill, for £175.1s.7d, describes it: 'neatly run with raised beads painted grey with arms in handsome ornaments, a beaded border round the Pannells, the Framing gilded, brass beads round the Leather, lined with fine light Colour'd Cloth, trim'd with Velvet Lace the same Colour, the Seat Cloth with one row of fringe, Plate Glasses to slide separately in front, Plate

Glasses and Mahogany Shutters in the Doors, an Oval Glass and Cushion to the back wainscott. Trunks under the seats, a Carpet to the bottom, hung on a light strong Carriage with Iron Axletrees . . . a set of upright Steel Springs . . gilded.' The curtains were of green silk, and there were six silk cushions. Fell, the tailor, made frockcoats and livery for the two coachmen, groom and postilion — James Trehearne, Francis Horne, John Batsford and Charles Evan. They wore light coloured coats and breeches, yellow striped waistcoats, brown surtouts and fustian frockcoats, and had gold epaulettes and gilt buttons. The bill for these clothes came to £52.17s.4d.

In the summer of 1778 other clothes bills were for uniform. Several pairs of doe skin breeches, strong shoes and regimental boots were bought. Mrs Hill ordered silver Shropshire militia lace, epaulettes, hatlace and loops, and buttons for her own military costume — the ladies attended the militia ball dressed in red like their uniformed husbands. Now, however, it was not just a matter of social occasions — France had entered the war on the side of the Americans, and the militia had to spend long periods in camps on the south coast. As their Lieutenant Colonel, Noel Hill had to take an active rôle. He did not neglect his estates, however, continuing to spend considerable sums on improvements, on building, and on repairs to tenants' houses, during the later 1770s.

Chapter 6
Lieutenant Colonel of the Militia

Shropshire feeling about the American war had been expressed in verse at the Caractacan meeting at Longnor in the summer of 1776, as reported in the *Gentleman's Magazine:*

> 'For other scenes, beyond the vast Atlantic,
> Horrid with arms, and stained with civil blood,
> The Muse with grief beholds, and with soft Pity's
> Mournful eye deplores, weeping the dire ills
> Of lawless Faction, blasting the fair fruits
> Which Freedom and true Liberty bestow'd
> In happiest climes, on those her fav'rite sons.
> Instead of regal sway, for gen'ral good,
> Fierce democratic rage usurps the seat
> Of Empire, spurning with rebellious pride
> The hand parental . . .'

It was not until after Saratoga that the danger seemed great enough to make preparations for home defence essential. On 28 March 1778 an order was issued to draw and embody 'with all convenient speed' the county militia, and to assemble on 13 April at Shrewsbury. It began its march on Thursday 7 May, as recounted by Phillips' *History of Shrewsbury:* 'The Shropshire Militia marched from Shrewsbury to Bridgnorth, where they were reviewed, and remained till June 12th, when they marched from thence to encamp on Cox-Heath, near Maidstone, in Kent, and on their route were reviewed by his Majesty in Hyde-Park, June 26th.'

Noel Hill had already been to Cox Heath 'to settle matters for the Reg'', as he wrote to his father from Worcester on 14 June, 'and shall go this evening to Bromsgrove where the Division I am to take is. I find the Major and all here in high spirits, the camp is on a High Healthy Heath . . . I was at the Levee the day Gen' Calcroft made his report to his Majesty and the aid de Camp was so polite as to shew it me. it was very particular and in the strongest and handsomest Terms, much more Complimentary and Flattering than even my Partiallity to the Reg' will permitt me, not to think was exceeding its Merit. I received great Civilities from Col. Frazier and other Officers of the Regulars in Camp in giving me every Information I stood in need of. The Duke of Grafton marched all the way at the Head of his Battalion of the Suffolks.' This new activity brought zest into the lives of Noel Hill and his wife; Mrs Hill would have to play her part, and it was with pride and excitement that she wrote to her father-in-law from London on 27 June. 'Dear Sir, as I am fearfull from the hurry Mr H: is in he may not have time to write to you by this night's post, and you may wish to hear of him I have the pleasure to inform you he is in perfect health tho rather grown thin thro the exercise and fatigue he has of late undergone. They were yesterday reviewed by his Majesty in Hyde Park, who expressed his greatest satisfaction with the Regiment, and I heard him repeatedly tell Lord Amherst who was on horseback with him, that the Regiment was infinitely superior to any he had seen both <u>under arms</u> and <u>in marching</u>. he was quite in spirits and pleased with it. I happened to be very near where he was and he was extremely civil and talked to me a great while about the Rejement and where I was to be, whether I went with it, what House I had got . . . he afterwards spoke to Lord Clive, but told <u>Mr H</u> that he knew <u>to whom</u> he was oblig'd for all the attention that had been paid to the Regiment, that he had seen none who so thoroughly understood their duty and was so well disciplined. he rode with them a good way and made all his inquirys of Mr H: and commended them beyond measure . . . Mr H: is at present in Town. he joins the Reg[t] tomorrow they will be in Camp on Tuesday and I shall get down to the Farm House which he has taken a part of, on Wednesday next, I shall have Tommy in Town tomorrow who will be vastly pleas'd with yr remembrance of him in the Shrewsbury cakes. I have promised him to come to us for a fortnight or three weeks to see his sisters at Coxheath . . . the children beg their duty to you.' In September she wrote again, her father-in-law's reply expressing pleasure 'to hear you have been visited and entertained by the chief of the nobility.' Her sister Jane Vernon was staying with her, and Lady Broughton and Mr Errington had visited.

Militia camps could be social centres of some brilliance — almost a holiday for some. They replaced the country season for the Hills for a few years. Lord Cholmondely gave a dinner in his marquee on Cox Heath for the Duke of Grafton, and the Duke and Duchess of Devonshire — the Duke was commanding the Derbyshire Militia. The one inn on the heath, and those in Maidstone, were filled with visitors. Something of camp life is recorded in a militia notebook of Noel Hill's. It gives details of the duties and regulations to be observed in the camp; routines for daily inspections, drawings of provisions, cleaning out of tents, and so on. The straw in the tents was to be dried out once a fortnight: 'A sunshine day should be chose if possible as also the Day the Men receive the straw.' Divine service was to be performed every Sunday, and prayers read three times a week at nine o'clock, at the head of each regiment. All surgeons were to keep a sick list and report to the C.O. every morning. The order for 15 June 1778 includes thanks to the Suffolk Militia for being cheerful and soldierly. On 13 August Major General Morris ordered that men of the Salop Militia should mess regularly and that an officer should visit their messes every day to see that there were sufficient quantities of meat and vegetables. A criticism by the General, on 17 August, that regiments were weak under arms, excepted the Yorkshire and Salop regiments. There were some courts martial, for desertion, and sentences of 1000 lashes; Bryan Sheridon, a private of the 18th Regiment of Foot, was to be 'shot to death' — the line turned out to see him pass to execution on 12 September. At Michaelmas the Hills were in Shropshire, where Noel was to be sworn in as Mayor of Shrewsbury. At the end of the year the Regiment went to their winter quarters in Dartford and Gravesend. Hill stayed at the Falcon in Gravesend and the Bull at Dartford; James Trehearne was with him, to take care of the horses. The Shropshires were on guard at Gravesend in the winter of 1778-9, suffering severe weather. The following spring they moved on.

Hill wrote to his father on 30 May 1779: 'I believe the Reg' marches on Saturday but it will be in cantonments for some little time before it encamps.' That was the summer when the older children were taken to Hastings. At the end of July Noel was given two days' leave to go to London 'on account of my Friend Major Boycott whom Col. Acland on hearing he was my Friend was kindly appointed to be Lt Col in his new Battalion.' He told his father there was 'not one word of News in Town which does not seem so much alarmed at an Invasion as I expected from the Continual Alarms we are kept in on the Coast, by orders and letters from the Commander in Chief . . . I was at Temple Bar where I met with their usual politeness . . I found by them that they were not much alarmed in the City.' The war was not going well: that summer Spain combined with France and some sixty or seventy enemy ships lay off Plymouth. They were content to cruise, however, until illness among the crews caused them to return home. Lord North's position grew weaker, and 'Wilkesism' revived. In the summer of 1780 the Gordon Riots occurred, bringing violence to London. The Mayor appealed to the Commander in Chief of the Army to send help, but this was difficult with so many troops in America. Regulars and militia camped in Hyde Park and prepared to defend the royal palaces, the Bank, Royal Exchange, Guildhall and Inns of Court. Confusion and terror prevailed one night, with deaths and fires. By 9 June the riots ended and Lord George Gordon was put in the Tower. Twenty-one rioters were executed. Parliament was dissolved on 1 September and in the subsequent election Noel Hill was once more returned for the county, this time with his cousin Richard Hill of Hawkstone. In the first few divisions of the new Parliament he voted with the opposition, as he had been doing since 8 March. In the spring of 1781 he visited Shropshire to deal with his own affairs: new buildings were put up for his tenants in Atcham and the old stables were turned into a dwelling for Abraham Cook and some of the 'very old Poor' whose premises had been pulled down. After dealing with other estate business he attended again to militia matters.

From London, on 3 June, Mrs Hill wrote on behalf of her husband to his father, to say that he was setting out that day on his journey to Devonshire; he was to be accompanied part of the way by Mr Errington who was going to visit his seat in Hampshire. The boys had been sent for a week before and were still in town. That year the regiment was camped at Roborough Down, in Devon. On the 9th Noel wrote to his father in Shrewsbury: 'I have been from hence to see the Ground we are to encamp on which is exceedingly good and to get a House for Mrs Hill. I have so far succeeded as to get one at a convenient distance but it only consists of a Parlour and a Kitchen with Four small Rooms above stairs and no Garrets so that it would have been impossible to have any of the Children with us . . . I am much hurryed in giving necessary Directions by letter to Mrs Hill in moving my Family of Children down to Tern, herself to me here and preparing myself for the March.' On 18 June he reported from the camp: 'On Monday the 11th I marched from Exeter with the first Division and on Tuesday encamped on this Down. luckyly that was a Dry Day since which we have had incessant

Rains and are wett through in only going from Tent to Tent, the second Division was obliged to pitch on wet ground and yet we are all very well. I dined with Gen¹ Haviland yesterday and am to dine with Gen¹ Grey this Day, they are both married men and I hear their Ladyes have assemblies in the Evenings but I believe there partyes are not yet begun . . . The road we marched here was over Dart Moor an extensive barren wild Forest and the weather has been so bad since that I have not had it in my power to see any of the fine parts of Devonshire.' The bills for purchases in readiness for this encampment give us some idea of life in the wastes of Devon for Noel Hill that season. From John Trotter, in London, he had purchased a large field officer's marquee, for £15, camp stools, a double headed couch, 'a very good hair Matras' and two bolsters, oil cloth (for a ground sheet), folding mahogany camp tables, two servants' beds and palliasses with bags to pack them in, and a canvas valise. From his bookseller, he bought notepaper and message cards, a copy of the Militia Act, Army Lists, Almanacks, Parliamentary reports, volumes two and three of Gibbons' *History of the Roman Empire,* and ink, pens and sand.

Conditions improved, and on 30 June Noel wrote that a week of fine weather had enabled him to ride out a few miles from the camp. 'The country at some little distance is very Romantick and Beautyfull. I have met with civility from Mr Heywood who was in the last Parliament and has a charming place about two Miles from hence; my neighbour in Town Mr Parker [John Parker lived at 29 Sackville Street] is expected down here this week, he has a fine House and a noble Place. the Camp being eight miles from Plymouth it is ill and not plentyfully supplied, the Mead bad, the officers fare rather better as we get Fish, the whitings which I like better than any are larger and better than any I have met with and not dear.' (A bill, dated 13 September 1782, for whitings, crab, shrimps, eels, salmon, one John Dory, a haunch of venison and 1½ dozen claret came to £12.18s.4d.)

Lord Clive — Edward, Lord Clive had succeeded his father Robert as lieutenant of Shropshire — had written, asking Hill to make his apologies to the regiment; he had gone with Lord Powis to Flanders to make a short tour, but would be with them the following month. The bad weather had done its work, however, and Noel and others suffered colds, swollen faces and agues. He also had gout, about which he wrote on 27 July, with that odd eighteenth century intimacy as though it were a tolerated familiar. The cold 'made the Gout fly about me for some time, it is at last come to one of the most kind fitts I ever had, it settled in my two feet and I have felt no further inconvenience than a little confinement and am much better than before it fixed, it has deprived [me] as yet of seeing Mount Edgcombe and other places. I have dined once with Mr Parker who lives superbly well, there was a large company, he desired me in future to come in the family way to him.' John Parker's mother had planned the extension of the Tudor house at Saltram by building around it, enfolding it in a graceful Georgian set of rooms. John Parker himself was a broadly spoken Devonshire man, but moved in fashionable London circles. From 1768 he had been employing Robert Adam who made a Saloon which, according to Nigel Nicolson, 'has no equal in the West Country and few elsewhere'. Ten years afterwards Adam converted the library into a dining room; the morning room was hung with portraits by Parker's friend, Reynolds. The Duchess of Devonshire was enchanted with the beauty of Saltram, and we can be sure that Noel Hill admired and studied all its features.

Thomas Hill was at Tern that summer and his son expressed the hope that he amused himself 'pretty well . . . and that the Children are not too noisy for you.' Thomas Hill had evidently wanted to send pineapples from Tern but his son dissuaded him: 'I should rather think it too far to send Pines here. If they are sent by the Coach I fear they will be heated as the last sent to London were . . . and from what I saw of them at Easter I do not think the Pines promised to be very fine.' By the end of July he was joined by his wife. On 9 August he sent further news to Tern. 'Mrs Hill has been here Ten Days and is much recovered since she came. She had a severe return of her fever after I left Town. I wrote to Mr Walker to consult with him who recomended her to get out of Town . . . She very anxiously followed his advice and has found the change of air the greatest service; she went down to Epsom to see the boys who were both perfectly well, Tom was grown quite fat.' His estates in Shropshire still needed his attention, the more so as Hurd was proving an uncooperative steward. 'I find it as difficult as you do;' he told his father, 'to get any money from him, I think he suffers the Tenants to run a long while in arrears after the Rent Day and is fond of advancing money to tradesmen on account which he says gains great credit but it keeps my pocket quite drained . . . I really keep myself quite Pennyless for the sake of getting the Estates which have been so long neglected in good condition which will be for the Benefitt of those that come after me.' Meanwhile, at Roborough, they were preparing to be reviewed by the generals next day, and were to entertain them to dinner afterwards.

On 27 August Noel wrote to say that the Fleet under Admiral Darby had returned to Torbay, bringing an account of the French and Spanish fleet — about forty men-of-war, some frigates, and several transports. One report said that this fleet was heading for the Channel, another that it had gone to Brest. The Duke and Duchess of Devonshire had again visited the camp, as had Lord and Lady Edgcumbe, who invited the Hills to Mount Edgcumbe. In September Noel Hill and Lord Clive made an excursion to Lands End, 'making the circle of Cornwall by the North and South Coast riding as near as we could to the sea. We had fine weather and the co[a]st is well worth seeing particularly Mounts Bay and Falmouth. At Pendennis Castle on the present alarms they were busy in getting up Guns on their new works. There as well as at Plymouth and other Places they stopped the Cartel ships and relanded the Prisoners from one that was getting under way . . . they are detained lest they should furnish intelligence to the Combined Fleets before ours sailed which passed by Plymouth this morning [15 September] consisting of 26 Sail of the Line.' He had been sorry to find, on his return, that Mrs Hill was again suffering from fever and ague; sea bathing was recommended: 'If it should be soon removed on this account as well as that of the present Critical situation I can not with any certainty speak of the time I shall be at Tern.' Ten days later, on 25 September, he wrote again to his father, now at his home in Abbey Foregate. 'I went one morning last week to pay my respects at Mount

Edgcombe and to make an apology for Mrs Hill to Lady Edgcombe for not having it in her power to wait upon her Ladyship again before she left this Country being advised not to cross the Water, it was luckyly the morning Sir George Rodney landed there, I never heard a man talk faster or in higher spirits he described our forces and Fleets to be superior both in the West Indies and America . . . Old Spain he said had lost New Spain forever, Tobago was of no value to us, St Lucia was a fine Healthy and Immensly Valuable Island to us . . . in short he represented this Country to be in a much more powerfull and prosperous situation than is quite credited here.' Mrs Hill had now been advised to leave Devon, and Hill hoped to be at Tern by the middle of the following week.

His father must have returned to London that autumn, for on 13 December Noel was writing from Tern about his father's wish to come into the country the next spring, and his fear that his Abbey Foregate house would be too noisy. Noel pressed him to use his house: 'as you would not think of travelling such wheather as this and not till Spring when my Family will all be gone to Town and Tern quite quiet I cannot see where you could be better and I am sure (as you ought to be) you would be heartyly welcome there and everything should be done as you ordered . . . There is to be a Grand Week at Berwick that is to say the House is to be full from Top to Bottom. We are invited for the whole week but have excused ourselves till Thursday on account of my cold, indeed Mrs Hill cannot bear a Week's raking, nor can I well be so long from home.' In Parliament in the spring of 1782 matters of moment were debated. The King had proclaimed a General Fast for 8 February, to solicit 'a special blessing in our arms' on account of 'the just and necessary hostilities in which we are engaged, and the unnatural rebellion carrying on in some of our provinces in North America'. Divine aid was equivocal: Rodney had a victory over the French in the West Indies, but the Thirteen United States of North America sent John Adams as minister plenipotentiary with letters of credence. George III also lost his prime minister when the Commons forced North's resignation. Thomas Hill made his last journey to Tern, where he died on 11 June. An announcement was published in the *Shrewsbury Chronicle*:

'Wednesday morning last died at Tern in the 89th year of his age, Thomas Hill, Esq; formerly a Representative in Parliament for this town, and Father of Noel Hill Esq; one of the Knights of the Shire for this county. Revered by his children, beloved by his grandchildren, and universally esteemed by his friends.'

Noel Hill had at last come into his inheritance.

As we have seen, he had been established at Tern since his marriage and had tried to improve not only the house but the estates and the houses of his tenants. He already had considerable status in the county and Tern was the heart of a community, and was itself one. The Hill family we know by name — Noel and Anne and their six children, Harriet, Tom, Anne, William, Richard and Emily, now aged six. At this period we can also put names to the household staff from two surviving lists, the second dated 1 December 1782. These give the people, their positions and their wages per annum. Board wages, varying from four to seven shillings a week, are in a final column; these were paid in lieu of keep when the family was not in residence or when the coachman and his like were on the road, or the butler in London. At Tern, Mrs Davenport was now housekeeper and Mrs Evans cook; at twenty guineas and twenty five guineas respectively their wages were slightly less than their predecessors', Mrs Skelton and Mrs Thorp. Isabella Thorp, kitchenmaid and possibly a relation of Mrs Thorp, had left, but Eleanor Jones remained and had been joined by Jane Vaughan — their wages were £4 10s a year. Molly Blockley looked after the dairy, at £4, while Ann Jones, stillroom maid, Jane Colley and Sarah Woodhouse in the laundry, and the housemaids Elizabeth Davies and Molly Palmer earned £6; another housemaid, Bridget Davies, got £7. The original four nursery maids had later been reduced to three and by this date only Molly Coventry remained, at £5 a year. Mrs Poignat, 'with young Ladies', was probably a governess, earning twenty guineas a year; Mrs Lloyd, lady's maid, received thirteen. The house steward, at the head of the staff, was still Richard Partridge, who was now paid £50, while Robert Marsh, the butler, got £40. Nicholas Rogers, under butler, and Thomas France and Richard Poole, footmen, were paid £14, as was Richard Oakley, the brewer. The first coachman, John Harries, got £18, the second coachman £14, the two postillions and two grooms £10, and the three 'helpers' a little less. The huntsman and whipper-in of Hurd's list had disappeared, and the 21 outside labourers were reduced to a dozen or so. The gardener was an important figure, earning £30 — in 1782 he was John Manderson. Many of the names are local, sons and daughters of estate workers and tenants, but some servants were recruited in London. The house at Tern, with a growing family and a sizeable staff, was becoming crowded. Some of the staff travelled from the country to the Town when the family did, the lady's maid and governess going in a family coach, while other staff had their coach fares and expenses paid, with places inside or outside according to below-stairs status.

Chapter 7
The Arts of Peace

Peace negotiations continued through 1782. The pattern of the seasons, for the last few years altered by the establishment of the militia camps on the south coast, could be resumed. But there were changes. Since the beginning of the American War, Parliament had had longer sessions, and sittings, and it was now customary for country members to be in Town for about a month before the Christmas recess, as well as after it. There was more business to be got through, so the House sat longer into the summer. These changes are found reflected in the account book kept by Robert Marsh, who succeeded William Bennett as butler. From mid or late January until April or May, depending upon the date of Easter, the household was in London. A brief stay at Tern was made over the Easter period, perhaps only by Noel Hill, to supervise estate business. From April to late June the family were still in Town, and the entertainments continued: visits to theatres, masquerades, assemblies, the pleasure gardens of Ranelagh, and the Pantheon in Oxford Street. The country season ran mainly from June to November, with the usual rounds of visits to and from friends, race meetings, hunts, and plays in Shrewsbury (Mr Miller reasserted his authority). The hunting activity changed somewhat for Noel Hill. From early in his attendance at the militia camps, he had given up part of his large pack of hounds — thirty-six and a half couple were sold to Thomas Jelf Powys — but Hill still went out with the Shrewsbury, and also hunted from his estate at Shenstone. Other variations in the itineraries came when two of his sons were at Rugby School, first William, then Richard; and with regular visits to spas: Scarborough, the Wells at Clifton, Buxton, and, from 1785, Cheltenham. One year there was a month long tour to Yorkshire, the Lake District and Lancashire. Reflected in this new pattern may be not only an interest in seeing other parts of the country, but increasing ill-health. Although a November visit to London became part of the annual round, Christmas and New Year were usually spent at Tern, in the old way.

Mrs Hill had long been a devotee of the theatre, often attending with her sister-in-law Lady Broughton. She was a subscriber to the venture of Harris and Sheridan, the *Opera* at the King's Theatre from 1778 to 1781. Sheridan had also succeeded Garrick at Drury Lane in 1776. This was a time of prolific theatrical entertainment, if not great drama; fashionable and unfashionable alike flocked to see the varied programmes: tragedy, comedy, farce, pantomime, combined in what seem to us odd juxtapositions — *Othello* followed by *Catherine and Petruchio,* for instance. Mrs Hill and her friends could have seen Garrick at the end of his career, and Kemble and his sister Sarah Siddons at the beginning of theirs. Sheridan's plays were very popular, and there were many other new plays, revivals, and Shakespeare. In the spring of 1782, when the account book shows much theatre-going, Drury Lane put on, among other plays and operas, *The Way of the World, Macbeth,*

The Tempest, The Provok'd Husband, Judas Maccabaeus, School for Scandal, Acis and Galatea, Hamlet, The Beggar's Opera and *The Duenna*. It was in that year that Sarah Siddons returned to London, to become a sensation as Isabella in *The Fatal Marriage*, Belvidera in *Venice Preserv'd*, the name part in *Jane Shore*, and innumerable other roles. One spectacular aspect of the Drury Lane productions was the magnificent stage scenery painted by Philip de Loutherbourg, and his admired effects of storms and clouds. A painter from Alsace, noted for his romantic landscapes, he was employed by Garrick and then Sheridan as scenic director at Drury Lane. The audience's taste for theatre found further outlet in the fashionable masquerades, where they could dress up as classical deities, exotics, or witty characters. Large private houses, theatres or the Pantheon in Oxford Street were venues for assemblies. Horace Walpole (designer of his own rococo Gothic house at Strawberry Hill) described the Pantheon in a letter to Horace Mann in April 1771. 'Imagine Balbec in all its glory! The pillars are of artificial *giallo antico*. The ceilings, even of the passages, are of the most beautiful stuccos in the best taste of the grotesque. The ceilings of the ballrooms and the panels painted like Raphael's *loggias* in the Vatican. A dome like the Pantheon, glazed.' In 1784 it was the scene of a notable concert.

The Great Handel Commemoration, held in 1784 — they were one year out in their calculations — was one of the most celebrated musical events of the time. Other performances, including a royally attended one, were given in Westminster Abbey. Dr Burney wrote an account of the composer and the event. In it he wrote of the special organ installed in the Abbey by 'the ingenious Mr Samuel Green, of Islington', who was paid £100. It was made for Canterbury Cathedral, but used in London first. This detail adds to our interest in Dr Burney's links with the Hills, for a few years later Noel Hill commissioned Green to build an organ for his Shropshire home. It has already been remarked that Charles Burney taught Hill's eldest daughter, Henrietta. He taught many fashionable 'Masters and Misses'; he wrote in 1780 that winter brought the routine of teaching: 'out every day before 9, & hardly ever at home before 11. What a Tourbillon is London to me at this time of the year!' Being taught by the great Dr Burney, and attending concerts and operas, did not necessarily imply a talent for or understanding of music, but the Hills had a genuine interest in this art. Henrietta was a very able pupil: she played the guitar (like her mother), the harpsichord and the pianoforte. Her ability may be inferred from a letter written to her much later by her former teacher. Burney offered 'more than a million of thanks . . . for the most kind, acceptable and splendid present of Sala's *Regole di contrappunto;* wch being the last and best book on ecclesiastical music that Italy has produced, I very much wished to possess.' As to her desire to pursue her former studies in Counterpoint, he was sending 'the first and only complete copy of Haydn's 6 Symphonies, wch I have been able, as yet, to procure'. (She had commissioned him to purchase this and paid the bill.) 'They are admirably printed, and the study of such scores will be more intelligible and improving to students in composition than a 100 dry treatises.' She was one of his 'musical graduates', who often made up a party to play. He also regarded her as a friend, remembering her in his will as one 'with whose

principles too strong for his ardour; she even fled abroad incognito to escape but his letters pursued her. He also wrote to her uncle, in June 1785: 'to you, my dear Errington, I address myself first as I have always dealt most openly with you in everything that related to Mrs Fitzherbert.' (Since her second widowhood, her uncle had acted as virtual parent, her father being incapacitated by paralysis; he looked after her brothers too.) Persuaded that she would be truly married in the eyes of her Church, she returned home; a secret ceremony in December was witnessed by her brother John Smythe and Henry Errington. Society was puzzled — were they married? Should one go to the opera with Mrs Fitzherbert? The Earl of Ailesbury wrote in his Journal, in May 1787, that he had seen the Prince in Mrs Fitzherbert's box at the theatre, and Lady Berwick and Lady Broughton in the Prince's box below.

In the summer of 1785 Noel Hill paid a first visit to Cheltenham. This spa was now becoming fashionable, the first Assembly rooms having been built in 1780. The waters were said to be effective for all bilious complaints, obstructions of the liver and spleen, loss of appetite, bad digestion, and the like. We know that Hill had a long-standing 'bilious complaint', but we do not know its exact nature. Each year now he would visit Cheltenham. There is a contemporary description of the town in the journals of John Byng. He stayed at Mrs Field's, Grove House, 'the best lodgings in the place, and nearest the well . . . detach'd from the town, and overlooking lovely meadows . . . The walks both public and private are shady and pleasant; opposite the pump is a new long room, where the papers are taken in . . . On Mondays there is allways a public breakfasting . . . There is a gaiety in a public breakfast in a summers morning, with music, that is to me very pleasing; every one then looks fresh and happy.' New rooms and a theatre were built about this time, to add indoor entertainment to the pleasures of outdoors — the walks beneath elms and limes, and the vistas of fields. In the autumn they were able to take up residence at Attingham, although it was not finished. Richard Partridge recorded that on 8 October 'My Lord dined in the new House at Attingham the first time', and on 10 October, 'Lady Berwick slept in the new House for the first time.' (Berwick had been chosen as a name from the hamlet on the estate, Berwick Maviston.)

The interior of Attingham was designed after the French manner, with wings leading from each side of the entrance hall, one 'masculine', the other 'feminine'. The entrance hall had scagliola columns, and behind was the staircase (this area was later altered, when the picture gallery was added by the second Lord Berwick). On the left of the entrance was the dining room, then the inner library, an anteroom, and the octagonal study; the west pavilion housed the outer library. The other wing consisted of the large drawing room, leading to a smaller one, an anteroom, and the boudoir; the east pavilion was the orangery. As we might expect of Steuart, the decorative schemes were especially striking: there was an Adam-style plaster ceiling in the drawing room, and the boudoir was exquisite with painted panels, doors and ceiling, and a French type chimneypiece, probably by John Deval the younger. (Many of these features may still be seen.) The smaller rooms would afford privacy, while the large rooms each side of the entrance would allow for public assemblies, for the Berwicks were now one of the leading families in the county. The Atcham ringers were paid for ringing when the family came down, and on the heir's birthday, in October. From early in 1786 work was done on the old hall by Richard Lee and his men, altering doors, taking down and removing furniture, fitting up a new butler's pantry, kitchen, scullery and larder; tables and forms were moved from the old servants' hall (possibly for the new way being made through the house to the inner courtyard). Richard Lee, the master carpenter who had done so much work on Tern, now had a dozen or more men working on the old house, two of them Lees, so they may have been his relations. They also made packing cases, troughs for the gardener, and pegs for a marquee in the latter part of June. Tern Hall was still used by the family, as well as for domestic offices; with six children to be accommodated, as well as guests, some of the old bedrooms were in use. Henrietta, the eldest child, was now sixteen, and the youngest, Emily, was nine. William wrote, years later, of 'the three bedrooms where I used to sleep in the Old house . . . one looking to the river and the other two in the Court.' He may have had bedroom, dressing room and study.

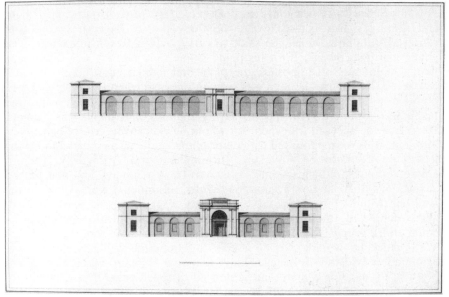

Steuart's drawing of the stables at Attingham. *(National Trust)*

Another important element of Steuart's designs was the magnificent stable block, also of Grinshill stone, with a great arched doorway and a fine range of stalls for over fifty horses. A few years later Hill had over twenty waggon horses, nearly as many hacks, five brood mares, several well-bred colts 'by Lord Pembroke's Arabian Ally Bey, Mr –'s Fearnought, and Lord Berwick's Catch'em which was bred by the Marquis of Rockingham, and got by Sampson out of Lapwing,' and Catch'em himself, who must have had a superior stall. Partridge's receipts mention the hunters' stables and the coach stables, and items of saddlery — side saddles show that the women rode too.

Races in August 1786 were attended, with William Jones as groom; entrance cost 10/6d, a stall at the course 11/6d, and weighing 2/6d. A Richard Jones was employed to bring the dogs home from coursing at Pulverbatch and Shenstone, and also at Poynton, Welbatch and Hadnall. Greyhounds and spaniels are mentioned; and two men were paid 5/6d for digging after a fox. Noel Hill was clearly intending to maintain his interest in racing and hunting. But he was as interested in his estate, introducing Dorset and Wiltshire sheep to improve the native Shropshire animals. There were cows, heifers and bullocks, and working oxen, and pigs. Attingham was a working farm as well as a gentleman's seat. Richard Burkinshaw, son of the former gardener, lived at the Home Farm in Berwick and played some part in the farm management.

In the summer of 1786 an unwelcome diversion was occupying Lord Berwick. On 21 June a young man rode up to Attingham and presented himself at the Old Hall, asking for the butler. He introduced himself as Thomas Knight, nephew of the innkeeper of the White Lion at Castle Bromwich. He was tolerably well dressed, with remarkably good teeth and a sun-burned complexion; he spoke with a broad Staffordshire accent. His news was that Lord Berwick's silver plate, which was being conveyed by Mr Powell's Shrewsbury waggon, had been stolen at Castle Bromwich; Knight and some servants had followed the thieves over Digbeth Bridge and retrieved the plate, which, he said, was now with a Rev Mr Spencer. The young man was rewarded for his pains. Some time latter it was discovered that 'Knight' was an imposter; the plate had indeed been taken, but not recovered. By chance the man was seen on the road when Lord Berwick was on his way to Cheltenham; he was apprehended by one of the servants and taken to Worcester gaol. There, saying that his real name was Thomas Horeditch, he accused four men, for whom he claimed he had only acted as look-out. Bills were published with descriptions of the wanted men, and many letters passed between Coventry, Birmingham and Attingham. Then it emerged that Horeditch was also known as Isaac Williams, and that he had changed his story: he now accused one Watts, a Londoner who lived near the Bull and Mouth Inn where the Shrewsbury waggon was regularly loaded. Watts denied the theft, produced alibis, and a London attorney whom he could afford to pay well. Lord Berwick was of the opinion that if he were on Watts' jury he would give no credit to Horeditch/Williams. Watts was acquitted at Warwick in August. Later that year Williams was committed at Stafford for stealing a mare and sentenced to seven years transportation to the eastern coast of New South Wales. He was to sail, after three years on the hulk *Justitia* at Woolwich, with the Second Fleet; he was on the *Neptune* whose master, Trail was a sadistic bully; 267 convicts of the Second Fleet died on the passage, 158 of whom were on the *Neptune*. We do not know what became of Williams, or of Lord Berwick's plate.

Work continued on the interior of Attingham and one important item was commissioned by Lord Berwick, for the drawing room. Designs by Steuart show organ cases as part of the decoration. The leading organ maker at this time was Samuel Green — the ingenious Mr Green of Islington mentioned by Burney in his book of the Handel Commemoration concerts. He had succeeded Snetzler as organ-maker to George III and built many important instruments after 1780. Elegant cases and a sweet tone were distinctive features of Green's organs. John Norman has written: 'Though lacking forcefulness in a large building, a Green organ is remarkably restful to listen to, an effect achieved with wide-scaled pipes gently voiced.' The Attingham sale catalogue of 1827 listed grand and cabinet pianofortes, a barrel chamber organ, and a 'noble brilliant-toned finger organ, by that celebrated maker, Samuel Green . . . in an elegant square panelled mahogany case, inlaid with satinwood'. Fortunately it was kept at Attingham and has recently been restored, and played, by Martin Renshaw who comments in his report: 'as it represents a considerable step in the evolution of the chamber organ, it must have been made for an enlightened and interested patron.' He praises its 'fine delicacy of voicing which is nonetheless rich and sonorous at its own low dynamic level . . . [it is] a uniquely preserved example of Green's mature work.' Having traced the Hills' interest in music, and the eldest Miss Hill's special talent, as well as the connection with Dr Burney, we can understand how Lord Berwick came to order the instrument. He apparently commissioned it in 1787 and it was completed in December 1788. Sadly, its patron would never have heard it being played.

We should say a last word about the architect of Attingham. Richard Partridge noted in his memoranda that on 9 July 1788 'St Chadds Church fell'. A committee was formed to choose a new site and an architect. They first decided on James Wyatt but he was busy and did not come to Shrewsbury, so they turned to George Steuart. He it was who recommended the new site — a stretch of town wall and a tower had to be demolished — and submitted plans. Eventually the committee agreed to the unusual circular plan of the new St Chad's: it too is neo-classical, with a four-columned portico and pediment; inside, Ionic columns support the gallery, and slender fluted columns rise from gallery to a painted and stuccoed ceiling, while two pairs of tall Corinthian columns flank the apsidal sanctuary — these are all white with gilded capitals. Steuart's work here is striking and original. St Chad's, with his church at Wellington, and Attingham, makes up an important group of the architect's buildings. Noel Hill's two elder sons, the second Lord Berwick, and William Hill, subscribed £100 'for St Chad's Bells', in 1798.

Chapter 8
Closing Scenes

The years which brought wealth and honours also brought troubles, especially to Anne Hill's family, the Vernons. Her brother Henry was living abroad, to escape his creditors at home. His wife Penelope having died, their son Henry, born in September 1779, was brought up by his mother's family in Ireland. The Grahams seem to have remained on good terms with Vernon, but there appears to have been an estrangement from his mother, Lady Harriet Vernon, for in her will she left him only the furniture and effects at Hilton (which was his patrimonial estate), and a few paintings.

Her own property, in various counties including the Wentworth homeland of Yorkshire, she left to her other surviving son Leveson. Her will was dated April 1779, some months before the birth of her grandson Henry, but it was not altered on his account. To her daughter Anne Hill she left £500, but made larger provision for her daughters Lucy and Jane, both unmarried. Lucy died in 1783 and was buried at Shareshill in Staffordshire, the church used by the Hilton household. All Lady Harriet's jewels had been left to Jane, except for a pearl necklace and ruby ring bequeathed to her 'Royal Mistress the Princess Amelia' — as we have seen, she was a Lady of the Bedchamber to this favourite daughter of George II, and aunt of the prince whose affair with Lady Henrietta Grosvenor had been such a scandal. Neither Henrietta nor Caroline, the Lady-in-waiting to the Queen, was mentioned in their mother's will. Lady Harriet died in April 1786 and was also buried at Shareshill; she had lived in London, in Grafton Street. Her son Henry was in the Crimea at the time, on a tour taken with a friend through Germany, Poland and Russia to Constantinople.

A letter written by Arthur Graham, to another son-in-law, Francis Lloyd, in February 1787, throws light on Vernon's situation. 'Vernon is with me [in Ireland], and very unhappy at the unkind and I may say barbarous treatment of some of his relations, particularly Lord Berwick, who has shook him off, and refuses to grant him any further supply or be any further concern'd in his affairs, if he does not desist from any enquirey into his mother's will, without giving any reasons but that such enquirey and pursuit is <u>unprofitable and iniquitous.</u>' There must have been a misunderstanding of what was probably sound lawyer's advice to his brother-in-law, for Lord Berwick was indeed helping Vernon. A copy of a letter written by Hill in 1785 to another impecunious Englishman abroad (a Major Feilding in Dieppe, a stranger who had written asking for £350) reveals Noel's habitual friendly and open nature. 'Having been frequently guilty of Imprudent Acts I ought to be the last man either to censure or not to forgive the errors of others. however my own have cost me a great deal of money, and I must acknowledge that the misfortune of many of my most intimate Friends and particularly those of a near Relation now on the Continent call frequently upon me for more Cash than I can conveniently spare.' Vernon returned to England on his creditors' signing a licence for his immunity, and Noel lent him £8,000. A Mr Woodcock was instructed to act for Vernon. Hill also seems to have taken an interest in affairs at Loton, though his old friend Charlton Leighton had died in 1784, to be succeeded by his half-brother Robert. Lord Berwick hired a chaise and pair on several occasions in the summer of 1788, from Robert Lawrence of the Lion Inn in Shrewsbury, to make visits to Loton. This activity on behalf of others continued through the year.

Noel Hill's health had been causing concern for some time. In January 1786 Sir Richard Hill of Hawkstone sent him a letter which included a reference to having seen him 'in great pain, and [I] have been apprehensive that you were in some danger.' (Despite his chagrin over the peerage given to a minor branch of the family, Sir Richard was a compassionate and Christian man.) Lord Berwick made another visit to Cheltenham in 1788, just after that made by the ailing George III. He was writing from the spa in September on behalf of the family of a Shropshire neighbour — Major Richard Grant, former owner of Berwick Maviston, who had died in July before being able to sell his commission. (There is a tablet in Atcham church to Richard Grant of the 11th Dragoons.) Lord Berwick was successful in his efforts as we see from a letter written to him by Joseph Yorke. 'His Majesty was graciously pleased to condescend . . . in favour of Major Grant's family. Having secured this capital point I must have recourse to your Lordship, who has so kindly patronized this family, to endeavour to prevent any disputes or difficulties in the distribution of the Money.' Members of the family wrote to express their gratitude to Lord Berwick. During December he was trying to stir the indolent Mr Woodcock into action on behalf of Vernon, but he was not to be troubled much longer by these family problems. At the start of the new year, at six o'clock in the evening of Monday 6 January, he died at his Portman Square home. Richard Partridge wrote: '1789 Jan 6 My Worthy Master the right Honble Lord Berwick departed this life. [Jan] 20 Attended my Lords funeral. His Lordship was Interred in the Family Vault [at Atcham] in the 44th year of his Age.'

Dying at the age of forty-three, Noel Hill had enjoyed his inheritance and his peerage, and his mansion, for only a few years, but he had done much for the status of his family. He was a well-off member of the landed gentry, but his income came mainly from estate rents and investments made by his father; he had no great mineral resources to exploit, no London property to develop, and no lucrative public office. The personal wealth accumulated by his father went mainly on building Attingham, and providing for his family after his death. Although half his time was spent in London, he was rooted in Shropshire, where most of his estates lay. He had served as M.P. and mayor for Shrewsbury, as knight of the shire and colonel of the county militia. His rural pleasures — racing, hunting, assemblies — were enjoyed mainly in Shropshire; and he had built his great house there. He was unlike many Shropshire gentry in having a permanent London home, and unlike many metropolitan gentlemen in remaining attached to a fairly distant county. In contrast to the brother who would have succeeded to the estates and wealth if he had lived, Noel Hill led a steady life, and was devoted to his family. For their welfare he had tried to provide when he made his will in June 1785. The rocks, torrents, and cataracts.' By winter they were all in Naples, with a notable English set, all enjoying the splendours and beauties of nature and the hospitality of the Hamiltons — there were weekly concerts at the Palazzo Sessa. Miss Hill, Harriet, seems to have been quite a favourite, enjoying the friendship of Lady Elizabeth Webster and Lady Sarah Plymouth, and earning the jealousy of Emma Hamilton. Italy was notoriously a place of dalliance, but Harriet's experience was both romantic and perfectly proper. We learn of it from the Rev Thomas Brand, tutor to the son of the Earl of Ailesbury, Charles Bruce.

Brand wrote letters to the Earl; in that of 15 January 1793 we find: 'Our weather at the beginning of the week was delicious though the thermometer was at the freezing point; which rarely happens, at least on the sea shore, but the last three days have been extremely disagreeable with violent storms from the Scirocco and Libeccio. We took advantage of the fine weather to carry Lady Berwick and her daughters to Cuma and Baia. The most eloquent pen could not do justice to the beauty of the views . . . ' He also had an incident to relate — 'it may perhaps have no small influence on our future life'; it happened on their excursion. 'Miss Hill and her younger sister were on horseback and gone on before, whilst the other sister and Lady Berwick were with me at some distance behind . . . Lord Bruce was with the former when on a sudden the horses began to plunge and kick at each other. Our dear charge spurred his and disengaged him from the combat, but Miss Hill's continued kicking and turning round violently with her. I expected every moment to see her dashed to pieces, when Lord Bruce jumped from his horse, ran with great intrepidity and presence of mind to her assistance, and came up just in time to receive her into his arms at the very moment when the pummel of her saddle broke, and . . . she was falling head foremost to the ground.' This tender moment, followed by the party's cold dinner 'on the southern terrace of a cottage which overlooked the Elysian fields', marked the start of a lasting love between the two. Brand told the Earl that he had a very good opinion of Miss Hill, 'who is of a very amiable disposition and sensible and conversible to a degree, which surprises me considering the great shyness and timidity of the rest of the family.' Lord Bruce wrote for his father's permission to propose — he was not yet of age; the Earl agreed and his son rushed to see Harriet and her family, who were all exceedingly happy. They were in Florence, Lord Berwick still at Naples; he sulked at not being in the secret and did not attend the wedding, though it was delayed a fortnight for him. (Harriet wrote him a very stiff letter.) They were married on 20 May. Lord Bruce commissioned Angelica Kauffmann to paint a portrait of 'dear Lady Bruce', crowned with roses and holding a lyre. Lady Ailesbury wrote to her daughter-in-law 'to express the sense I have of the Happiness you are the chief instrument of to my Dear Son who since he has been blessed with such a companion appears to have a more thorough enjoyment of Life than he ever experienced before . . .'

In the spring of 1794 twin daughters were born to Lady Bruce, but only one baby, Maria, survived. Lady Berwick, Anne and Emily were there, and her mother's presence must have been a great comfort to Harriet as they were very close to each other. A year later they were all in Germany, the Bruces on their way home. Another daughter, Augusta, was born in Hamburg; Lady Berwick was again with Harriet, having come from Ratisbon where she and Anne and Emily were spending the summer. (In the autumn a son was born to Henry Vernon and his second wife; he was named Frederick William Thomas and thirty years later he was to marry Augusta Bruce.) Lady Berwick was very sad to part from her daughter and the babies, but she did not want to face an English winter, and Anne was reluctant to return — Emily would be happy anywhere. Thomas Walpole, English minister at Ratisbon, gave them a farewell dinner in November, and after a fortnight 'always travelling' they were in Venice. Lady Berwick wrote to her dearest Harriet, hoping that she and the children were well; Anne wrote with news of the concerts at the Fenice. Venice was as bad as London for Lady Berwick's health, and they moved to Milan. The problem was where to go next; a visit to the Lakes would be pleasant, but the armies were in the vicinity. This was the spring when Napoleon made his offensives in Piedmont and Lombardy — he entered Milan on 14 May — and on into the Veneto. The ladies went to Rome where they visited their friends Lady Knight and her daughter Cornelia. Then they went to Naples, but most of the English visitors had left. 'Montagu Wilkinson . . . is gone to Ancona,' Lady Berwick wrote in October, 'still a safe road and from thence embarks to Trieste, this is the best plan of all because it is attended by the least <u>sea</u>, and the Adriatick is safe just now from Corsairs.' Lady Berwick was longing for England: '<u>if</u> there was a general peace we cd go home just at our own time in the spring with the summer before us . . . Your letters make me so happy in giving me so good an account of the dear Children . . . yr Sisters desire their most kind and affectionate love in which I beg to join with the same to Ld B[ruce] and the dear Babys, ever my Dearest Dear Harriet your most truly affect. Mother. I long so to see you whenever I think about it.' Peace did not come, and they were isolated in southern Italy. In the spring Lady Berwick did try to get home, anxious for her daughters and her own health worsening. She aimed for the Adriatic route, through Apulia, but she died there on 23 March 1797. Lady Grosvenor lamented the 'cruel loss of the most affectionate of Sisters, dearest and best of friends.' Harriet was distressed to learn of the circumstances of her mother's death: 'whilst I believed the event to have happened at Naples . . . I had the comfort of <u>believing</u> she had advice [and] every assistance'; she was concerned as to how her mother's body could be 'decently and <u>properly</u> convey'd through a large tract of country almost uncivilized'. Anne and Emily, and Barbara (a companion in their travels, probably Lady Berwick's personal maid), must be consulted about her mother's wishes. But these were clear, in the will that Anne Berwick had made over three years earlier, in November 1793.

'I hope my Dear Children will not consider this my last will and Testament as a partial one. I have but little to bequeath, I therefore leave the principal part of what I have to those who it appears to me will be most in want of it after my Death, but I wish to leave a token of my sincere Love and affection to all my Children and hope they will consider the trifles I am only able to leave to each as kindly and as affectionately intended to them as if the value was equal to my wishes which are greatly indeed beyond my ability.' The tokens included miniature pictures: to Thomas Noel, one of his father, 'the only original picture of him in the Family'; to her 'dear son in Law', Lord Bruce, one of his wife Henrietta and her sisters. To Harriet she left 'an enamelled ring set round with brilliants, with a large brilliant in the center and inclosing my Mother's Hair with an Inscription of her Name round the setting'. Legacies of £100 were left to William and Richard, and the rest of her belongings, including jewels, and money owed to her by Lady Grosvenor and others, were for Anne and Emily. They were also to share anything due to their mother from the estate of her uncle, William Wentworth, Earl of Strafford, who had died in 1791. If it exceeded £5,000 the surplus should go to her younger sons. 'I thank all my dear Children for their good and affectionate behaviour towards me which has contributed to lessen all my troubles and increase my comforts and happiness. It is my particular request to be buried as privately and with as little expence as possible. I likewise desire to be buried wherever I may happen to dye, that is, as near to the place as a protestant may be allowed to be Burried — shd I dye in a Catholick Country. I hope this request will not be considered as disrespectful to the Memory of my Dear Husband or my Family, as I am of the opinion that it is of little consequence where our mortal parts are deposited, and I look forward to the meeting of our spirits in a better World than this I leave.'

In accordance with her request, she was buried near the small port of Manfredonia — far from home, far from Atcham where her husband was buried, and from Attingham, which they had enjoyed so briefly. The great house stood largely unlived in, but it was visited, as Miss Plymley (sister of the Archdeacon) recorded in her Diary for 1794. In the summer of that year, after dining with Mr Burton at Atcham, the Plymleys 'in the evening walk'd to Attingham and look'd over Lord Berwick's magnificent house. It is a vast pile of building, built at great expence by the late Lord, who died very soon after it was completed, before some of the apartments were quite finished, it has scarcely been inhabited by the family yet. The present Lord, though fond of it, having hitherto been principally abroad — the sum it cost I am told was certainly not less than 50,000£.' The house still stands, overlooking the Tern, a reminder of past lives and of those whose portraits may be found in its elegant rooms.

Sources and notes

The main source of this work are documents in the Attingham Collection, the property of the National Trust, housed at the Shropshire Record Office, S.R.O. 112. Out of this large collection of letters and other documents, those mainly used are: Thomas Hill's letter books, 21 (1740-1753) and 22 (1753-1759); Thomas Bell's letters, boxes 20 and 23; letters of Noel Hill and his wife, boxes 26 and 42A; other family letters, box 31; vouchers etc. in boxes 39-42A. Rentals and account books have also been used. Additional documentary material is listed in the following notes.

General works consulted include: *Victoria County History of Shropshire,* III; Morris's 'Shropshire Genealogies', several volumes (Local Studies Library Shrewsbury); the *Histories* of Shrewsbury by Phillips and by Owen and Blakeway; Shrewsbury Burgess Roll; Joseph Morris's articles on 'Provosts and Bailiffs of Shrewsbury' in *Transactions of the Shropshire Archaelogical Society; Dictionary of National Biography; Gentleman's Magazine; Complete Peerage;* Burke's *Peerage, Extinct Peerage, Landed Gentry.* Other sources are given in the notes.

Chapter 1

The papers of the Hon. Richard Hill, Attingham Collection, part 1. John Nichols, *History and Antiquities of Leicestershire,* vol. IV, part 2 (1811), for details of the Noel family. William Noel's daughters Anne and Elizabeth predeceased Susanna and Frances; in his will, 1 Feb 1762, he divided his estate among the two surviving daughters and his nephew Edward Lord Wentworth. The Hills' Leicestershire estates came from the Noels.

Ann Hill's letter to her father, 4 Oct 1743: S.R.O. 112/B94.

Mrs Hill's undated note to Thomas Hill: S.R.O. 112/A146.

The letters of Anna Maria Leighton to her mother Mrs Barnston: Cholmondeley Collection S.R.O. 1536 box 5. A simple diagram may help identify the Myttons and Leightons mentioned in the narrative:

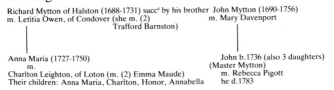

Richard Mytton of Halston (1688-1731) succ⁴ by his brother John Mytton (1690-1756)
m. Letitia Owen, of Condover (she m. (2)   m. Mary Davenport
                    Trafford Barnston)

Anna Maria (1727-1750)   John b.1736 (also 3 daughters)
m.   (Master Mytton)
Charlton Leighton, of Loton (m. (2) Emma Maude)   m. Rebecca Pigott
Their children: Anna Maria, Charlton, Honor, Annabella   he d.1783

John Fletcher's letters are in the Methodist Archive, John Rylands Library, Manchester. A forthcoming article in the *Proceedings* of the Wesley Hist. Soc. will deal more fully with Fletcher's time at Cleveland Court and Tern.

An account of Tern Hall, 1701-1775, will appear in the *Proceedings* of the Shropshire Archaeological and Historical Society.

Bonnell's letters to Thomas Hill: S.R.O. 112 box 24.

Chapter 2

Admissions to the College of St John . . . Cambridge, Part III, ed. R F Scott; D A Winstanley, *The University of Cambridge in the Eighteenth Century* (1958).

The Duke of Newcastle's Papers, B.M. Add. MSS 32925/32926, British Library.

James Bonnell's letters S.R.O. 112 box 25.

According to George Morris, MS 27, Local Studies Library, Shrewsbury, the Shropshire Militia was raised in October 1762 and called out for exercise October 1763, to serve for three years. The eight companies were commanded by the Earl of Bath, with one colonel, one lieutenant colonel, one major, five captains. Their uniform was scarlet faced with buff; in 1766 it was enlarged to ten companies, and the uniform was changed to scarlet faced with green.

The date of Noel Hill's admission to the Inner Temple confirmed by the Librarian and Keeper of MSS, Honourable Society of the Inner Temple, London.

Details of Sir Watkin Williams Wynn's tour: Wynnstay MS R40, National Library of Wales, Aberystwyth.

Details of Noel Hill at Edinburgh supplied by the Librarian of the University.

Chapter 3

The best background study is Lucy S Sutherland's *The East India Company in Eighteenth Century Politics* (1952). Details of Clive's elections from the transcripts made by Dr J F A Mason, from letters in the India House Library, for *VCH Shropshire,* vol. III. I am grateful to Dr Mason and to the present editor for making these available. Other Clive letters: S.R.O. 112 boxes 16 and 24.

I am grateful to Cherry Ann Knott for bringing Lady Mary Coke's *Journal* to my attention, and for a useful exchange of information about the Vernons.

For details of Henry Vernon's time with the 'Blues': P.R.O. Army Lists, WO 17/3. Other details from C J Apperley, *Nimrod's Hunting Reminiscences* (1843) and W Pitt, *A Topographical History of Staffordshire* (1817).

Details of the trial for damages brought by Lord Grosvenor from the *Gentleman's Magazine,* July 1770.

Chapter 4

Estimates and bills from Thomas Leggett: S.R.O. 112 box 41. I am grateful to Keith Goodway of Keele University for information about Leggett's commissions at Eaton and Chirk. Details of Wynnstay: Wynnstay MS R39. Mylne's business diaries are in the R.I.B.A. Library, London; I am grateful for the Librarian for her help.

Details of the chimney pieces from MS notebook, American Institute of Architects — copy in The Local Studies Library, Shrewsbury.

I am indebted to Sir Michael Leighton of Loton Park for information about the Leighton family and Loton, and for permission to reproduce the portrait of Charlton Leighton.

Information about the Caractacus Society was kindly supplied by Dr Paul Stamper of the *VCH Shropshire*. Corbett's diaries: S.R.O. 567 box 41.

For a history of the Jockey Club, Roger Mortimer, *The Jockey Club* (1958).

The description of Edward Maurice (by that time Mr Corbet of Ynysmaengwyn) is from *Richard Fenton's Tours of Wales 1804-1813* ed. John Fisher (1917).

Details of horse races from the *Sporting Calendar;* copies of the 1775 Calendar kindly supplied by the Eaton Estate Office, Grosvenor Estate, Chester. Extra details of the Holywell Hunt races supplied by Mr A G Veysey, County Archivist, Clwyd Record Office. Noel Hill's letter to Nicholas Smyth, and the 1769 list of Shrewsbury Hunt members: Cholmondeley Collection S.R.O. 1536 box 5. Other details from notes on the Shrewsbury Hunt minutes made for *VCH Shropshire* vol. II, made available by the present editor.

Information about the Worcester Music Meeting kindly supplied by the Worcester Record Office. An account of the meeting in 1773 is in *Origin and Progress of the Meeting of the Three Choirs of Gloucester, Worcester and Hereford*, by Rev D Lysons, J Arnott *et al.* (1895); the quotation is on page 50.

Thomas Bell's will: Lichfield Joint Record Office, Staffordshire. The Diocesan Archives at St Chad's Cathedral, Birmingham, were also consulted; my thanks to Fr. Dennison.

Richard Partridge's notebook is at Attingham.

Chapter 5
The account of the Shrewsbury election 1774: MS 2526, Local Studies Library, Shrewsbury (who have kindly supplied the illustration also). Other details from *Shrewsbury Chronicle* 1774. The 'Song in Commemoration of 19th November': MS 371, Local Studies Library. The quotation concerning Pulteney will be found in *VCH Shropshire,* vol. III, page 271.

The Earl of Derby's letter is in *Intimate Society Letters of the 18th Century* ed. the Duke of Argyll (1910).

Henry Vernon's letter to Smyth: Cholmondeley Collection S.R.O. 1536 box 5. For 'Records of the Corporation of Oswestry' see *Transactions of the Shropshire Archaeological Society,* 1879-1883. My thanks to Mr D J Preston, Town Clerk, and to Oswestry Town Council for allowing me to see the Race Cup and lending the photograph of it.

The Shrewsbury Borough Quarter Sessions, Jan 1777: S.R.O. 3365/2369. Details of Fishery meetings from the *Shrewsbury Chronicle*. Correspondence concerning the Bill: S.R.O. 112 box 41. *Statutes,* 18 GIII, c33 (1778).

Chapter 6
Noel Hill's militia notebook is in the Attingham Collection, S.R.O. 112. The description of Saltram House is from Nigel Nicolson's *Great Houses of Britain* (1978).

Details of the opening of Parliament: *Gentleman's Magazine.*

Chapter 7
The sale of Hill's hounds is mentioned in *VCH Shropshire,* vol. II, p. 168.

The description of the Pantheon, Horace Walpole, *Letters to Horace Mann* (1843).

Two works by Charles Burney have been quoted from: *Account of Musical Performances . . . in Commemoration of Handel* (1785) and *A General History of Music* (1789). Other works consulted: Roger Fiske, *English Theatre Music in the 18th Century* (1973) and Henry Pleasants, *The Great Singers* (1967).

Mrs Montagu's comment is from *Mrs Montagu . . . Her Letters and Friendships* ed. Reginald Blunt (1923).

R and G Steuart's account book for work at Portman Square S.R.O. 112 box 42A.

Details of Rugby School kindly supplied by the Librarian, and from Alicia C Percival, *Very Superior Men* (1973).

The account of the masquerade is quoted by H A Tipping in his article on Attingham, *Country Life,* 5 February 1921.

Details of Mrs Fitzherbert from various biographies and from the Earl of Ailesbury's Diary *H.M.C.* 15th Report, Appendix part VII.

The description of Cheltenham is from *The Torrington Diaries of the Hon. John Byng* ed. C B Andrews (1934).

Details of Attingham are to be found in articles by Tipping, *Country Life,* February 1921; Michael Rix, *Country Life,* October 1954; and the National Trust Guide to Attingham. John White's notebook: R.I.B.A. Drawings Coll., Portman Square.

Details of the animals are from the *Shrewsbury Chronicle,* April 1789.

Details of the theft: S.R.O. 112 box 42A; additional information from P.R.O. Stafford Assizes. ASSI/2/25; and the Australian Documents Publication, *The Second Fleet Convicts* (1982).

Comments on Samuel Green quoted from John Norman, *The Organs of Britain* (1984) and from the report by Martin Renshaw, kindly made available to me.

For new St Chad's, see booklet by P F Norton and Mary Hill, *New St Chad's and its Architect.* Receipt for subscription to bells S.R.O. 112 box 45, 16 July 1798.

Chapter 8
Lady Henrietta Vernon's will: P.R.O. 1151/149. Noel Hill's will: S.R.O. 112/129. Letter from Arthur Graham to Francis LLoyd S.R.O. 103/5/17.

Dates of burials of Lucy Vernon and Lady Henrietta from Shareshill parish register, Lichfield Joint Record Office, Staffordshire.

The letters in the Attingham Additional Collection (Ailesbury) have furnished much information for this chapter. Brand's letters to the Earl of Ailesbury, *H.M.C.* 15th Report, Appendix VII. Edward Clarke's letters home are quoted in *The Life and Remains . . . of Edward Daniel Clarke*, Rev. William Otter (1824).

Plymley Diaries S.R.O. 1066.

THE HILL FAMILY TREE

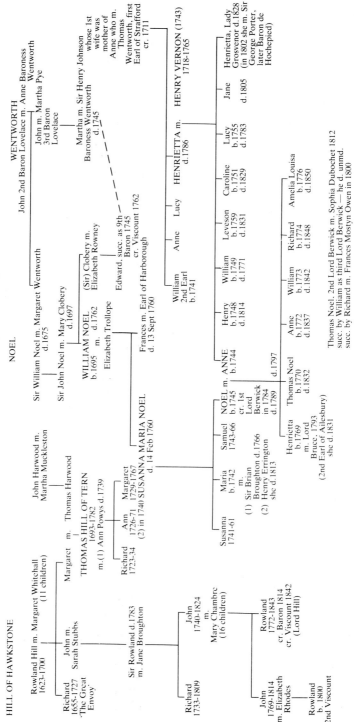

Index